The British Art Show 1990

24 January - 11 March
McLellan Galleries, Glasgow

30 March - 20 May
Leeds City Art Gallery

14 June - 12 August
Hayward Gallery, London

The British Art Show 1990

A South Bank Centre exhibition sponsored by 3i

THE SOUTH BANK CENTRE 1990

Exhibition organised by Caroline Collier assisted by Lesley McRae

Hayward Gallery showing organised by Greg Hilty assisted by Lynne Richards

Education and public programme: Helen Luckett

Film and audio visual technician: Jem Legh

Artists' biographies compiled by Sotiris Kyriacou

PHOTOGRAPHIC ACKNOWLEDGEMENTS:
Prudence Cumming Associates *51, 67*   Daniel Faroro *107*   John Gilmour *101, 109*   Catriona Grant *65*   H Kosanivic *73*
Susan Ormerod *45, 53, 69, 83, 85, 87, 111, 113, 115*   Bill Stephenson *101*   Peter White, FXP Photography *79*
Edward Woodman *37, 47, 55, 59, 63, 89, 99*

Catalogue designed by Arefin and Arefin
Assisted by Ian Hawkins
Typesetting by Spencers, Clerkenwell
Colour origination by Service 24, Brighton
Printed in England by EGA, Brighton

Text © 1990 The South Bank Centre and the authors

ISBN 1 85332 054 4

COVER: IAN DAVENPORT *Untitled* 1988 (detail) fully illustrated on page 51

A full list of South Bank Centre publications may be obtained from:
The Publications Office
South Bank Centre
Royal Festival Hall
Belvedere Road, London SE1 8XX

Contents

Lea Andrews

Eric Bainbridge

Black Audio Film Collective

Sonia Boyce

Jyll Bradley

Kate Bright

Melanie Counsell

Matthew Dalziel

Ian Davenport

Grenville Davey

Cathy de Monchaux

Jeffrey Dennis

Willie Doherty

Mona Hatoum

Kevin Henderson

Gary Hume

Kabir Hussain

Bethan Huws

Callum Innes

Brian Jenkins

Patrick Keiller

Joanna Kirk

Elizabeth Magill

Lisa Milroy

John Mitchell

Locky Morris

Julian Opie

Cornelia Parker

Vongphrachanh Phaophanit

Fiona Rae

David Robilliard

Caroline Russell

Veronica Ryan

Lesley Sanderson

Louise Scullion

Yolande Snaith

Gary Stevens

Linda Taylor

Peter Turley

Shafique Uddin

Rachel Whiteread

Caroline Wilkinson

Sponsor's Foreword

As Chairman of 3i, Britain's foremost venture capital group, I am delighted to support one of the most innovative exhibitions of modern art ever to tour in the United Kingdom.

Innovation, be it in art or industry, is a theme close to 3i. Like industry, art must take paths that lead in new directions. Only if there is a boldness, a willingness to take risks and an opening of minds to what is unfamiliar, will we make lasting achievements.

It is appropriate then to focus on the work of artists in their 20s and 30s working in Britain now to provoke thought and discussion and, most importantly, to stimulate new endeavours. Already, 3i has witnessed the power of imaginative thinking with the current renaissance in British enterprise.

Arts sponsorship is but another reflection of the 3i philosophy of helping to realise potential in more ways than one — by investing in both industry and the arts.

SIR JOHN CUCKNEY

Foreword

The British Art Show has a history, or, if that is too grand a term for a period of just over a decade, at least it has a family. This is the third in a series of large-scale exhibitions that have taken place at five year intervals and have looked at recent art in England, Northern Ireland, Scotland and Wales. The previous *British Art Shows* were different from each other in character and this one is distinct from them both. What has linked them all, apart from their size, is the emphasis on extensive, first-hand research and on the recognition of the need to visit artists up and down the country in order to base the exhibition on an awareness of what is happening in art all over the United Kingdom.

The 1979 exhibition, which was seen in Sheffield, Newcastle and Bristol by 77,000 people, was selected, heroically, by one person. The exhibition was intended to give a broad survey of recent activity and to allow for less familiar artists as well as established figures. William Packer, the artist and critic, was asked to choose what he considered to be the best of current art in Britain and he selected 112 artists, mainly painters and sculptors. The second *British Art Show* was even more ambitious in its scope: it was conceived as both a representative survey and an interpretative summary of a period. In recognition of the extent of this brief, it was decided to invite three people to devise the exhibition: Marjorie Allthorpe-Guyton, Alexander Moffat and Jon Thompson. Their exhibition brought together eighty-two artists and artists' groups and, as well as painting and sculpture, it included performance, film and video art and work using photography and mixed media. It was a Herculean task and was immensely popular: there were over 160,000 visitors in Birmingham, Edinburgh, Sheffield and Southampton, remarkable attendances for an exhibition of contemporary art in Britain.

Art does not, of course, comfortably fall into five-year periods and the first question we asked ourselves when beginning to plan this exhibition was whether a survey show would be an appropriate response to the conditions in art at the beginning of the 1990s. The 1984/5 exhibition had been thorough and it had occurred at a time when the 'New Spirit in Painting' and a reassessment of attitudes towards metaphorical language in art, which had swept Europe, were making themselves felt here. The repercussions were varied and interesting, for younger artists and in terms of the re-interpretation of the work of artists who had already established a way of working in an earlier atmosphere, less receptive to the eclectic interests of the 1980s.

It would have been impossible to have organised a survey of the major achievements of the period from 1985 to the present without including many of the artists who had participated in the previous exhibition. Naturally their work has evolved; but it did not seem worthwhile to duplicate the recipe for an event which had been the response to another time, with other needs. Many of the artists whose work would be included in such a broad survey have been seen together again and again since 1984 in shows abroad, and although this in itself is not necessarily an argument against showing them together here, the time is right, at the start of the 1990s, for a fresh look at the current situation. The two 'tendencies' amongst younger artists which have been made most visible in Britain in the 1980s are an expressive kind of figurative painting, perceived as emanating from Scotland (summed up in *The Vigorous Imagination*, which took place during the 1987 Edinburgh Festival) and the 'New British Sculpture'. The 'New Sculptors' are a loose group of artists who have responded to aspects of Modernist sculpture and to the possibilities opened up by an associative and referential language; they were well represented in *Starlit Waters: British Sculpture, An International Art, 1968-1988*, the retrospective exhibition that opened the Tate Gallery in Liverpool in May 1988.

In February 1988 we held a meeting to discuss the form the next *British Art Show* might take, with members of the Advisory Committee to the Exhibitions Department at the South Bank Centre, which included the artists Michael Craig-Martin and Alison Wilding and the critics Lynne Cooke and Richard Cork, David Alston from Sheffield City Art Galleries and James Bustard from the Scottish Arts Council. It was decided first that the next exhibition in the series should be exploratory — not a historical summing up of a period but a forward-looking exhibition which would suggest emerging possibilities by focusing on new developments. A notional age limit of 35 was suggested, in order to direct attention to lesser-known artists, and as a way of considering some of the young artists who have already established reputations in the unfamiliar but sympathetic context of the work of their peers. We agreed that the exhibition should not pretend to be a neutral survey, and for clarity it was decided to limit the number of artists participating to about 40 but not to reduce the scale of the exhibition, so that artists could be represented in a little more depth than is often possible in large group exhibitions, where there is a danger that individual pieces may become token examples, rather than being perceived as part of a whole body of work.

Having decided, in broad terms, the nature of the exhibition, it was crucial to choose the selectors to work with the South Bank Centre's Exhibitions Organiser Caroline Collier. Andrew Nairne, Exhibitions Organiser at Third Eye Centre, Glasgow and David Ward, the artist, who teaches on the degree course at Goldsmiths' College, were recommended to us as individuals and as a team for their knowledge of the wide area to be covered by the exhibition and for their support and understanding of young artists. An exhibition of this kind involves considerable commitment, in terms of time as well as energy, thought and imagination and they have responded very generously to the challenges, occasional frustrations, trials of physical and mental endurance of the last 18 months. This kind of project is particularly demanding on a practising artist and we are therefore especially grateful to David Ward for his unselfish consideration of others' work.

We are pleased that the exhibition is to start in Glasgow where, under the aegis of the City of Glasgow Museums and Art Galleries and with the support of the Scottish Arts Council, it will open the newly renovated McLellan Galleries as the first major exhibition in the city's year as Cultural Capital of Europe. We are grateful to the Scottish Arts Council and to Glasgow 1990 for their help and encouragement from the outset. The exhibition then travels to Leeds City Art Gallery, which has a long-standing tradition of support for innovative twentieth-century British art, reflected in its collection and in its own exhibitions programme. The third showing will be at the Hayward gallery — the first time a *British Art Show* has come to London.

We greatly appreciate the support of the exhibition's sponsor 3i. The company has shown a remarkable interest in the development of the project and an enthusiasm about the work of young artists in Britain. It is unusual to secure major sponsorship for an exhibition of contemporary art, particularly a challenging and speculative exhibition such as this one. We were delighted when, in recognition of this innovative and imaginative support, the sponsorship by 3i was given an award under the Government's Business Sponsorship Incentive Scheme.

Finally, we would like to join the selectors in thanking the many people who gave their help and advice in the preparation of this complex exhibition. We are very grateful to the lenders and to the artists, many of whom have made works for an exhibition which we hope will make a stimulating contribution to art in the 1990s and will open up the debate, rather than attempting to be the final word.

JOANNA DREW

Director, Hayward and Regional Exhibitions

MICHAEL HARRISON

Assistant Director, Regional Exhibitions

Selectors' Introduction

Our work, in selecting this exhibition, was a response to a positive, forward-looking and open-spirited brief to make an exhibition of the work of about 40 artists, focusing on those up to 35 years old in 1990. Work in all mediums was considered and we pursued every avenue available to see work that was new or unknown to us while keeping in mind that this is a curated exhibition requiring research and not an 'open' show.

Before the work of individual artists was even discussed, three simple ground rules were agreed between us that remained integral to our thinking, throughout the selection.

We endorsed completely the commitment to devote this large-scale exhibition to the work of younger artists. However, we remained flexible on the issue of age and tried to keep in mind the various circumstances and conditions that may affect the emergence and development of an artist's work. In the event, the large majority of artists in the exhibition are now under 35 and we have not included those who have less than one year's experience of working after graduating from art school.

We all expressed the view that the exhibition should not either be approached or structured on the basis of thematic sections. This is both a reflection of our individual perceptions of the diversity of work being made now and a shared resistance to the practice of selecting art to illustrate pre-determined positions. The debate and the thinking surrounding this view have probably most influenced the nature of the exhibition as a whole.

We were all sceptical of the need for, or usefulness of, a comprehensive 'survey' exhibition. This exhibition does not embrace a retrospective view of acknowledged achievement but it is an expression of what is, only now, being made visible.

The exhibition does not attempt to define national traits in art; it reflects only the 'Britishness' of a multifaceted and multicultural society. We have intentionally been as inclusive in our selection procedure as possible. Only a very few artists who will be in the exhibition were on all our minds from the start and it has been for us all an exploratory process, based on extensive research and the advice of many people. We have seen and considered, in various ways, work by over 1,000 artists. In the past year we have made studio visits all over Great Britain and in Northern Ireland. Despite our efforts to ensure that we considered the whole of the United Kingdom inevitably a high proportion of the selected artists now work in London, although they have migrated there from all over Britain and from abroad.

Not surprisingly, we have found that there is no single, prevalent, movement or style and the much discussed 'pluralism' — in the sense of varied attitudes and approaches to the making and the content of work — is reflected in the diversity of the selection. We have found ourselves continually questioning meaning and value and how convincing a work is in relation to the artist's situation, within the complex framework of the late 1980s. Originality, in terms of a search for the 'new', has not been an overriding concern but the sense of the particularity of an artist's use of visual language has been a guiding principle.

There is a degree of trust expressed by an artist to show work in such a context that should not pass unacknowledged. There is also a responsibility that exhibition selectors and curators have to artists and for this exhibition that extends to every artist considered, whether or not their work was eventually included in the exhibition itself. It was a valuable and extraordinary experience to be given an opportunity to see so many artists working now in Britain, particularly at a time when art schools are suffering financial cutbacks and a number of fine art departments are being closed. The exhibition can only give a glimpse of the energy, imagination and resourcefulness of young artists. We hope that, as an exhibition, it will come alive in the minds and imaginations of those who visit it.

We have worked closely with the participating artists, who have been very generous in their attitude to the project. We have intentionally avoided trying to assume an 'objective' stance in our work on the exhibition and this is reflected in the publication, which includes the voices of most of the artists as well as contributions from each of us.

CAROLINE COLLIER
ANDREW NAIRNE
DAVID WARD

I. In the air

This exhibition brings together the work of over forty artists. Very few of them have ever exhibited work together before and, for all the participants, a large number of the other artists in the exhibition were, until now, completely unknown. For the artists themselves therefore, as well as for visitors to the exhibition, this is an unfamiliar gathering. No themes were pursued in selecting the work, no theoretical stance preferred and therefore the exhibition as a whole embraces considerable diversity — it is an exceptionally varied milieu within which to find even familiar faces.

It has been said that every viewing of an art work is in some way a first viewing and it is certainly true that to see the same work in different circumstances can transform it, or rather our experience of it, sometimes subtly, sometimes considerably. Within a group exhibition individual works are also seen in an interactive relationship (occasionally resonant, perhaps uncomfortable) with other works in the exhibition.

An exhibition such as this involves considerable preparation and research. And yet it does not exist until the works themselves come together in the gallery for the first time. No amount of forethought and planning can anticipate the actual apprehension and coexistence of the works themselves. Even as a selector, at the time of writing, I have seen the work only in the individual artist's studios, often weeks or months apart; sometimes in progress, occasionally in the context of other exhibitions and a number of works will only exist as proposals until they are actually made for the first time within the gallery spaces.

As the selection of the exhibition developed I attempted to keep one principle in mind: to avoid forming generalisations about the work, the practice and the predicament of individual artists. Generalisations are useful but where we rely on impressions we risk losing sight of the particular and actual, for generalisations are invariably taken from the surface of experience. An exhibition is frequently seen as an event, bounded and contained, easily attached to fixed meaning. How we perceive such an event is not necessarily synonymous with how we may experience the art within it. A concern of this exhibition is to allow the art itself to become visible, rather than be obscured by the surrounding event: for the parts not to be subsumed by the whole.

These reflections express some of the ways in which this exhibition seeks to remain a fluid, unfixed project. Nevertheless this is a definite stance, a position intended to return us to the particular in the work of these artists and it is an attitude that reflects directly the extraordinary diversity of art being made now.

What then, is in the air? In relation to art this expression is often used perjoratively, to imply the fashionable, the temporal and insubstantial. It is, more positively, an expression that suggests the intangible, the idea of concerns, issues and influences that make up an atmosphere in which elements are identifiable yet not fixed and which are reluctant to be pinned down.

Naturally (or predictably), a question frequently posed during the selection was whether an emerging new tendency or movement is detectable: anticipation of new movements places an emphasis on what is about to occur, in the future, next in art, rather than focusing attention on what is present now. My response remains unchanged — that whatever constituents there might be circulating in the air a new orthodoxy has not crystalised. Indeed, 'pluralism' now seems an inadequate word to describe the present extent of diverse practice; the absence of a prevailing stylistic hegemony or dominant set of conventions or axioms; the dissolving of international styles and the re-investment of forms and languages with new meaning and life.

II. Without Walls

How we understand this dynamic condition of almost bewildering diversity and put it into context depends in part on changes in attitudes to, and the interpretation of, the history of art which is related both to broader concepts of history and to ideas of perception.

The subject of history is a central philosophical concern. The debate, from Kant to Foucault, has manifestations on many cultural levels and we gravitate towards the future during a period in which the concept and study of the past itself is undergoing continuous scrutiny and redefinition.

Now, at the beginning of the 1990s, it is difficult to remain immune to the excited anticipation of the significance of the approaching years. After all, this is not only the passing of one more decade. We have entered the ultimate decade of both the century and millennium.

We are witnessing the social and political transformation of central and Eastern Europe and the

Soviet Union, a protracted process dramatically signified by the demolition of the Berlin Wall, a contemporary icon as powerful as the destruction of the Bastille two hundred years ago. Breaching the wall has tremendous symbolic importance but the implications and consequences of the changes taking place are not contained in that single historic act. It is timely to be reminded that Mao Tse Tung, when asked what the full significance of the French Revolution had been, replied that it was too soon to tell.

That remark reveals an attitude at odds with conventional perceptions of political history that tend to abstract linear sequences, one event leading to another in a continuous causal development towards the present. Art history is conventionally structured in a similar, horizontal, linear pattern in which artists and the concept of the masterpiece have an equivalence to major events in social history.

These interpretations of historical change are founded in a nineteenth-century idealism, based on an industrial revolution, rationalist philosophy and empirical science. As such these views serve a utopian idea of continuous progress and improvement in which the roots of the progressive avant-garde in art are found. But even the description of the development of the avant-garde greatly oversimplifies the complicated interactive relationships between artists, in an attempt to impose at least a retrospective logic on art. This fixes art, as if historians and critics were cartographers identifying landmarks in vague terrains.

Indeed the image of landscape is a recurring metaphor. Umberto Eco, in the *Aesthetics of Thomas Aquinas*[1], describes the examination of the historical as the ascent of a tower to raise one above the surrounding landscape. Eliot employed the metaphor rather more dynamically in *Tradition*[2], describing, for example, the critical appraisal of art in which the relative stature of artists continuously changes as they recede, so to speak, in the perspective of a landscape of time. For Eliot this was a flexible process, always liable to be revised, and he goes on to develop the proposition that the art of the past not only contains within it potential for new art, but that, importantly, new art can also transform our perception of art that preceded it.

This concept of a responsive relationship between new art and the art of the past emerges in André Malraux's text *Musée Imaginaire* (or *Museum Without Walls*[3]) which represents part of his attempt to dissolve orthodox art historical categories. Responding to the ubiquity of photographic reproductions of art and, I am sure, to Walter Benjamin's ideas concerning the implications of mechanical reproduction in art, Malraux conjectured, controversially, that all art, of all periods and places of origin, becomes available, transformable and contemporary through reproduction. The museum, such a recently invented institution, no longer has walls and yet, as Eliot said of art history, nothing is lost.

III. There is more under the floor [4]

The sculptor Richard Wentworth has also used the metaphor of landscape to describe his own working sense of history but he has moved significantly away from the image of a receding plane to the sense of depth beneath our feet:

'History, I think, is probably like a pebbly beach, a complicated mass, secretively three dimensional, and very hard to chart what lies up against what, and why, and how deep. What tends to get charted is what looks manageable, most recognisable (and usually linear) like the wiggly row of flotsam and driftwood, and stubborn tar deposits'. [5]

These lines provided me with a fresh insight into the renowned Situationist slogan of Paris 1968: 'Underneath the paving stones lies the beach.' — that below a carefully dovetailed and continuous surface lies a shifting texture of unresolvable complexity and potential.

The distinguished scholar of the seventeenth century Christopher Hill, with a certain oppositional edge, remarked recently:

'The most fruitful change in historical attitudes in my time has been the emergence of 'history from below' — the realisation that ordinary people also have a history. History no longer deals exclusively with Kings and their mistresses, Prime Ministers and wars . . .' [6]

There is an underlying optimism to all these images that relates to the recent redefinitions of historical change that I touched upon earlier. The past is no longer regarded as a given sequence of fixed events representing constant values that project us into the future. Rather history is a construct that we constantly remake, the better to understand our present.

When in *Ulysses*, Stephen Dedalus said 'History is a nightmare from which I am trying to awake' [7] he also spoke for Joyce's own position as an artist. For *Ulysses* is at once a modern work intimately bound both to a classical model and to Irish history. If for Joyce history assumed the metaphor of dream then what could he desire to awake to if not the present of conscious experience? This is not a present in denial of the past and (although for Joyce there was, I think, a strong element of historical inevitability) the suggestion is towards freeing oneself through knowledge and experience. Such aspirational thinking does not (to pursue the metaphor of the Odyssey) rely on being able to anticipate one's course or destination. More recently, Michel Foucault, articulating the idea of philosophy as the art of thought, spoke of the intellect constantly seeking to unsettle its own habits of thinking — the capacity to aspire to depart from known experience and through this to realise and recognise, perhaps, a sense of return and actual presence in the world. (Foucault described this sensation with characteristically qualified optimism as both 'comfort and dismay').[8]

These are ideas of an essential fluidity in our understanding of our relationship to history and tradition. The imperative of progressive development and the concept of immutable, absolute values or essences being embodied in art are continuously dissolved or sceptically questioned and this has parallels in areas of scientific study.[9] The implication of research in physics now bears directly on our understanding of perception. That we are active participants in experience and not merely the observers of constant and objective phenomena has a special resonance with our engagement with art. Evidence in physics that conditions of observation affect the behaviour of that which is observed actively engages and integrates us with the world. While both science and art may provide us with models of reality, art may also involve us directly in experience of which we are potentially an inseparable part and which need not, finally, be mediated by word and language.

'So language scatters the totality of all that touches us most closely even while it arranges it in order. Through language we can never grasp what matters to us, for it eludes us in the form of interdependent propositions and no central whole to which each of these can be referred ever appears. Our intention remains fixed on this whole but we can never see it in the full light of day. A succession of propositions flickering off and on merely hides it from our gaze, and we are powerless to alter this.'[10]

DAVID WARD

1. Umberto Eco: *The Aesthetics of Thomas Aquinas*, Radius, 1988.

2. T.S. Eliot: *Tradition* — from *Selected Prose*, Penguin Books, 1953

3. Andrew Malraux: *Museum Without Walls* — from *Voices of Silence*, Princeton University Press, 1978

4. Parkett Art Magazine: (There's more under the floor), advertisement for Parkett, Zurich

5. Richard Wentworth: *The Sculpture Show*, Arts Council of Great Britain, 1983

6. Christopher Hill, *Lies About Crimes*, The Guardian newspaper, May 29 1989

7. James Joyce, *Ulysses* pg 31, The Bodley Head, 1937-49

8. Michel Foucault: *The Regard for Truth/An Interview*, Third Text No 16, 1984-5

9. see Thomas Khun, *The Structure of Scientific Revolutions*, The University of Chicago Press, 1962-70
   and Ilya Prigogine and Isabelle Stengers: *Order out of Chaos*, William Heinemann, 1984

10. Georges Bataille, *Eroticism*, Calder and Boyars, 1962

Climate

Here, in temporary relation, are artists of such different backgrounds and outlooks that to seek to package them together neatly, to build theoretical barriers, would result from, or produce, critical dementia. It is inevitable, in an exhibition of this kind, that interrelationships will become apparent but these may be momentary coincidences, which soon redistribute themselves into another pattern. Art is a part of a complicated web of experience and isn't a hermetic activity, separate from the variegated happenings, trivial and profound, that make up the texture of our lives. All the artists here are singular and independent, in that they are inventing or adapting visual language, so that it means something particular to them, now. It seems to me that in this attempt at making a genuinely contemporary, challenging art there is optimism: a willingness to look outwards and forward.

Inventiveness in art frequently involves making visible things which have been disregarded, unseen or previously unknown — or the showing of familiar things in a new light. It only takes a small change of focus, a slight shift of interest or emphasis, the concentration on a detail, an examination of something that has been marginal, to bring about a re-ordering of our experience, a need at least for re-adjustment. We are not cut off from our personal or collective past and it isn't surprising that many of the artists here are working in a more or less direct relationship with the major movements in Western art since the Second World War: Abstract Expressionism, Pop Art, Minimalism and Conceptualism. But this exchange is coloured by a sense of the complexity and fluidity of the present and very recent past which has bred a mistrust of generalisations, dominant ideologies and grand abstractions, and an attraction for the particular, the local, the apparently inconsequential, for the fleeting and chaotic — for all that resists the 'mainstream' of linear progress. The 'post-modern' world has been shaken up a bit by the awareness of other voices, distinct from the established order. This may be one of its most positive aspects, notwithstanding worries about decadence and the 'colonisation' of experiences belonging to those whose cultures and attitudes are other than our own.

The unfamiliar is uncanny. We can't quite recognise it and so, in relying on appearance, we may be likely to misplace or misconstrue what is at first only a notion. In looking at artists' work during the last year, it has struck me how curious it is that an object may resemble some other thing but have quite a different meaning. The container, although physically it defines what is within, does not always betray its contents. Surfaces, immediate appearances, are important but even after close attention they do not reveal everything and what might seem to be a tendency can draw into itself disparate positions and sensibilities. What happens, for instance, when we bring together in our minds the fragile surface of one of Callum Innes's white paintings, the result of a cumulative process of mark-making, partly dissolved; the instantaneous pearlised sheen on the packaging of Caroline Russell's cotton wood buds; the gleam on the ersatz pelt which covers Eric Bainbridge's sculptures; the ivory-coloured stuff which appears to be the substance (but is only the coating) of Grenville Davey's *Right 3rd and 6th*, molars whose roots seem to go deep into the insentient gum of the gallery walls; and the gloss skin on one of Gary Hume's magnolia paintings, which resist being gazed at to the point that the shapes in low relief give you back a rudimentary face or death's head with empty eyes? A point in common — in this case simply and superficially an absence of strong colour — hints at the distinctiveness of each artist's outlook.

The issues of 'authorship', of personality and the control the artist has over the relationship between the viewer and the work of art are live ones. After the supposed demise of the author[1], a crisis of the 1960s, the question of authenticity still appears to be a compulsive part of the discussion surrounding new art. This inescapably involves the concept of originality, even if the artist intentionally denies such a position and adopts a self-conscious stance of anonymity. In the 1960s some younger artists in America felt their own situation to be remote from the gestural sincerity of Abstract Expressionism and aimed to make work in a way that brought the viewer into a direct relationship with ordinary, mass-produced things, having emptied out the personal, heartfelt involvement of the Artist-Creator. In the 1980s, painting of an expressive kind has seemed most dominant, but conditions today are quite other and there cannot be, as a reaction to this, for any young artist now, a 'return' to Minimalism or to any other phase. It is axiomatic that the past is continually re-interpreted, according to the needs of the present.

Nonetheless, in their questioning of the relationship between the artist and the viewer, and in allowing the person experiencing the work to bring to it his or her own interpretation, some artists working now are investigating, for their own purposes, aspects of the language of earlier Minimalist artists, whose work has sometimes been accused of being empty, cold or, in terms of some current thinking, domineeringly 'corporate' and sexist. Other artists here are reinvesting different languages with fresh meaning — for instance an expressive figuration, or abstract expressionism, or a kind of painterly realism, or academic life drawing. But for each, the significance, the originality, is in the specific use to which the visual language, of whatever kind, is put. The work resists being categorised according to its appearance and will not be pinned down by an analysis of its style, or even of its medium. Some of the works are hybrids. This seems especially true of the 'installation' works and of the performances by Gary Stevens, which mix the conventions of theatre with sculptural concerns, and those of Yolande Snaith, where dance is used as a medium for embodying ideas and feelings.

Some artists are finding that spare, minimal forms, things which might look 'pure', can reverberate with associations. Mona Hatoum's grid *The light at the end* is a simple structure, a beautiful and sinister object. Above it the light on the walls makes a pattern resembling an angel's wings (a fallen angel?). The meaning is rooted in sensation: the shock at the sight of the rods of fire, the feeling of a warmth which is not comforting. Yet it is only electric fire elements suspended in a dark space, as, for that matter, a painting, which offers us an internal world, is at the same time only the stuff it is made of.

The sense that meaning is defined by the process of making the work is strong in this exhibition — for many of the artists the activity of working is exploratory and in some sense intuitive, so that ideas may occur as a result of practical and mundane decisions, rather than being predetermined. There is an ordinariness, a matter of fact quality in this attitude which is antithetical to the adoption of any subservient position in relation to theories surrounding art. What could be less remarkable than the space under a kitchen table? Rachel Whiteread's sculptures are utterly honest about what in reality they are — castings from furniture; so that the invisible, the air, is made substantial. At the same time they seem to withhold secrets, to contain messages — traces of the people who have sat around the tables, perhaps, or, independent of their source, they are tombs, boxes, caskets: containers for private feelings and thoughts. *Yellow Leaf* refers to the table's flap and to death, to the dwindling of light and warmth, to winter. It is an associative object, with metaphysical dimensions.

The way to admit references and to embody them in the physical presence of the work is a preoccupation of many younger artists. Their work is inclusive of a range of experiences and interpretations, from the metaphorical implications of Cathy de Monchaux's pinning and fixing of pliable material with metal clips, bolts, bands, zips, and nuts, which has lead to a reading of her work as 'fetishistic', to the way that water evokes human presence in Melanie Counsell's installations. These suggest our common predicament as fallible beings, whose efforts at a cosmetic cheerfulness and decoration may underline the pathos of an inner stagnation. Our experience of this work is not contained, as it might tend to be when we gaze at an object: we are enveloped by the atmosphere of the work, by its palpable presence, even to the musty smell of the roll of old carpet, rotting like the corpse of a sheep in a stream.

Most of the works in the exhibition resist being stared at in a passive manner, they encourage our active engagement, an alertness of our senses. A painting, a photograph, a sculpture, a film, a live work, is not there just to be glanced at but to be explored in the mind and imagination, to be turned around, questioned, examined from different angles. Bethan Huws's little boats of rush, placed in vitrines, may suggest that the artist puts on display the most intimate, delicate details of a past which is not ours to share. Made, perhaps, to float in a stream in some remote place, what are they doing in a gallery? The artist does not see them as 'art', they are too close to her, but these tiny crafts, like the fragile barque in the Breton prayer[2], may suggest hope and the predicament of being solitary, that each of us has an individual fate. They are barely there, but they are concrete things which suggest to me the 'specific reality' of images and the power that they have to communicate directly with us, as individuals, on the level of our daydreams, so that we cease to look outwards but draw on our own private store of memories. [3]

The 'communicability' of actual things, natural and man-made, as triggers for memories and associations, seems to be at the heart of this exhibition. It connects Grenville Davey's strange, fabricated objects with Cornelia Parker's haunting arrangements of trophies, Eric Bainbridge's hirsute, massively enlarged sculptures and Kabir Hussain's tiny bronze slivers of tracts of landscape, one of them as small as a well-sucked toffee bar, Julian Opie's secular, maze-like construction and Linda Taylor's Celtic cross, which is a sort of contemporary Dream of the Rood, an outward, physical form for a spiritual experience: for a transfiguration which does not come in a flash but is slow, organic, apparently tentative and as ineluctable as new spring shoots on a tree. For an instant, the impulse towards correspondence seems to link all the artists here. Then, specifically, memory, where language as a rational system ceases to work, appears central to Vong Phaophanit's *Fragments*, where photographs of the artist's distant family are projected onto a screen of shimmering air, so that the work in sculptural, physical terms, embodies the essence of memory. It seems to operate in Shafique Uddin's drawings, where images resolve themselves and dissolve in dabs and flashes of colour and light, where the surface of the board becomes like that moving screen of air. It is present in Caroline Wilkinson's *Interior*, where the camera's exploration of a room becomes an examination of the workings of an inner world and in Black Audio Film Collective's *Twilight City*, where London is perceived as the site for personal experiences, for small, individual fates.

Memory is not the past but involves the bringing of things into a kind of 'eternal present', it makes the subconscious real, suggesting that truth is always subjective. Lisa Milroy isolates the objects in her paintings from the confusion of their ordinary surroundings, and this seems to draw attention to their specificity as objects, which may also be variously emblematic, and to their arrangement on the white screen, plane, or ground of the canvas. We are aware of the duality of paint — where a touch of pigment remains just that at the same time as it is, for instance, the individual bow or fastening of a shoe, or a frosted glass flower on a light bulb, or a little piece of an image printed on a stamp. Have the objects fallen, or drifted, into such configurations or has someone put them precisely there? The pictures may be partly about artifice and arrangement but they recall too the apparently random disposition of things in the natural world. The objects in the paintings are at once mundane and open to interpretation, to be contemplated for what they may reveal to us of our own attitudes. Works of art, in stimulating our desire for significance, for relating this with that, continue to imply the possibilities suggested by Proust, that great explorer of the capacity of memory to reveal the relative truths of experience, in his comments on reading:

As the result of a curious but providential law of our mental vision (a law perhaps which means that we can never receive the truth from anybody but must always be creating it for ourselves) what is the end of [the author's] wisdom inevitably appears as the beginning of ours. [4]

Is art then in some sense anonymous or is it drenched with the personality of its maker? I do not see any of the work in this exhibition as merely 'personal'. But it is evidence of the transformation of what is significant to the artist into some strange, new, external thing which may release in the viewer other experiences and meanings which are in turn specific to him or her and may be more or less private. This is not to deny the social aspect of art, or its inextricable entanglement in the 'context' of the culture in which it is made. On the contrary, the implication is that artists, in following through what strikes them as being of interest, are able, paradoxically, to make something which takes on an existence that is quite independent of the vagaries of temperament and which may have a direct bearing on a range of issues and concerns, whether or not the work is 'issued-based', as the term has it.

For some of the artists here, personal predicament is the starting point for an exploration of wider issues, so that what might appear to be 'self expression' is in actuality strategic. Brian Jenkins's use of an expressionist kind of drawing is directly related to his own physical state: not only are the charcoal drawings self-portraits but they are made in extreme conditions, so that the drawn marks delineate the extent of his occupation of a space. His photographs of landscape, exquisite in themselves, and within a recognisable tradition, are poignant because they portray places that a person disabled physically is more or less prevented from entering. Brian Jenkins's photographs can be related to Willie Doherty's, which are made with an awareness of the same idealistic tradition of landscape photography, and where again nothing is innocent, where barriers and barricades between people are set up.

Lesley Sanderson's self-portraits, made in the analytic manner of academic life drawing, are strange and confrontational, subverting their style. The artist gazes out, challenging prejudice. Making the personal political, (an attitude which has been discussed in relation to black and feminist art) has its dangers. It may give away too much of the artist's privacy, allowing the viewer to be a voyeur. This invasive tendency is recognised by Sonia Boyce, whose earlier drawings depicted herself, her personal history, and members of her family. The new works using photography and photocopying as well as drawing, are attempts at putting domestic details at a remove while continuing to explore ideas that matter deeply to her and are, in their impulse, intensely 'personal' and felt.

The tone of David Robilliard's paintings, which, like his poetry, use phrases that seem to have been snatched from the filofaxes of advertising copywriters or from the jingles of D.J.s and at other times refer to the language of enchantment, to fables and stories, is sometimes lyrical, occasionally abrasive, intentionally challenging and unsettlingly obscene: their content is almost invariably an expression of the position of being homosexual in Britain in the late 1980s. The question of tone is vital too in Lea Andrews's photographic works, where the artist, mock-heroically and comically, poses in the guise of sculpture which commemorates the non-existent official history of the outwardly insignificant, rootless place which contains his own most private memories of childhood and adolescence. The matter of the disjunction between personal and formal versions of the past and between individual identity and nationality reverberates through an exhibition which includes the voices of people whose histories and values may be at odds with the prevailing social order.

In a culture so lavish in its production of objects and images, the point of making anything else, or new, has appeared elusive to some artists. This was one of the foundations of Conceptualism and the idea of the mass circulation of popular images is of course at the root of Pop Art. Ideas of representation in this exhibition suggest to me the possibility of finding points of reference in the many-layered reality of the present and are at a remove from the seamless 'hyperreality' of simulation, which is undoubtedly an aspect of our world and which has been written about so persuasively and imaginatively by Baudrillard that his ideas have become a kind of orthodoxy, giving rise to a new academicism of 'signification'. Naturally, Baudrillard himself, with his restless curiosity, is continually reassessing his position and defies the fixed meaning given to his perceptions by some of his followers. One of his most evocative images, certainly in relation to Britain in the 1980s, is the enclosed shopping complex, that place of desire, excess and fantasy, where crowds of people, drawn by the spectacle as much as by the activity of buying anything 'useful', drift about in an 'unreal' world which is remote even from the variations of the seasons, in a 'perpetual springtime' of climatic control.[5]

The irregularities and idiosyncrasies evident in this exhibition suggest some reappraisal of our relationship not only with nature but with the artefacts of our culture. Although a diversity of sources, mediums, styles and attitudes is the characteristic, none of the artists has simply 'appropriated' and re-presented material. A transformation has occurred in the way that ordinary things, unaltered in themselves, have been put together — as for instance in the work of John Mitchell, where boxes and packing crates are brought into relation with advertising bill-boards, forming new systems of communication, or where images, normally invisible, have been revealed — as in Matthew Dalziel's installation *Unseen, Unheard but Measured*, which suggests the hidden correspondence between high and low tech, between natural and man-made organisational systems and structures, as well as the speed with which we, in the form of corporations, can colonise the planet.

This era of the 'post-modern' has taught us to look carefully and sometimes hysterically at the most outwardly insignificant things, to 'decode' the seemingly innocent. What does that Benneton advertisement of the brightly clad multi-cultural children reveal to us? Academics and philosophers have turned their minds to the study of the ostensibly trivial, and artists have drawn our attention to what would otherwise seem negligible. Peter Turley's paintings transform ephemeral, disregarded things into the stuff of high art. Large paintings based on the designs on paper which has wrapped meat confront as with images which imply a questioning of our dominant position within the natural order. Our consumption of other living things and our subjection of them to our will are symptomatic of our consumption of everything — from images to the world's resources. The 'animal' paintings speak to us of ethics and of the imagination — the very things which, to our shame, distinguish us as human beings from our fellow creatures.

Jeffrey Dennis's pictures, which, like Lisa Milroy's, make a new kind of realist painting, draw into themselves and give internal logic to multifarious ways of filtering experiences and information — through film, television, still photography, with the naked eye, through a magnifying lens, in a mirror, condensed into the flat pattern on wall-paper or opening out into the long prospect of a street, every conceivable relationship to reality can be remade in paint. In one small picture, through an enlarged undergrowth of individual stalks and blades of grass in which lie mouldy plums, we peer down at a street where tiny cars are fixed like bugs on a stem. Are we looking at a robust picture of ripeness and purpose or are these fruits left unharvested after some incident such as Chernobyl? Have the cars too been abandoned? This unpeopled autumn picture is curiously ambiguous about the contemporary significance of that ancient symbol the horn of plenty, bringing together fruits of nature's and of man's productivity.

The laws of the internal world of the work of art and the rules, accidents and probabilities of everyday life seem to be flouted in Fiona Rae's paintings, which have an absurd relationship to the Modernist idea of the Artist as Magician. Sometimes the forms in the paintings are invented, or her sources may be as various as reproductions of paintings by Picasso or Kandinsky to images of frying pans or toys from an Argos catalogue. Her paintings are displays: the canvas is an arena where anything might happen. The flat surface becomes a sort of circus rink and the painted marks perform acrobatic feats or juggling tricks, turning, balancing, behaving clownishly or occasionally pirouetting elegantly. The artist seems to put the paint through its paces but remains disengaged. Ian Davenport's paintings too could be discussed in relation to the language of Abstract Expressionism; but when the artist's emotions are intentionally distanced we are left with a form into which can be projected other concerns. The artist creates the initial conditions for a chaotic system which follows natural laws, so that a theme is determined by the behaviour of the paint. The pictures could be interpreted as jokes; comments on the gesture of self-expression, but this would not take into account their beauty, which consists partly in their relationship to what are almost meteorological conditions: to currents of air, to forces of gravity, and partly in their relationship to spaces in which we can wander imaginatively, fictional domains where gnarled and twisted tracks of pigment may be reminiscent of the roots in an Arthur Rackham drawing, or where you are confronted by a form which may resemble a cliff-face, some Gordale Scar, or simply an immense enamelled radiator. They are at once mock-heroic and genuinely ambitious, absurd and fantastic, so that our desire for grandeur is stimulated while it is undermined. Romanticism is also an aspect of Patrick Keiller's film Valtos, a journey northwards from London through Mrs Thatcher's Britain, which has become transfigured, where the variable light of an unpredictable summer, given to overcast skies and sudden flashes of startling brightness, is translated into the curious luminosity of black and white film, and where the camera wanders about vagrantly, upsetting any predetermined conceptions about where the landscape ends and the imagination begins. A contemporary version of the pathetic fallacy (the identification between psychological states and nature) becomes a sort of molecular exchange between kinds of chaos, in the human mind and in the world at large.

The present is not the climate for prefabricated definitions, for the labelling of styles or movements, and in any case new art is particularly unsuited to this. The danger is that any attempt at fixing meaning may bring about the translation of something which is in essence exploratory and tentative into the alien terms of classification and category. The question of locating order in apparent randomness, always a concern of artists, has recently become a much-discussed preoccupation of science. The ubiquitous 'chaos theory' can be read as the celebration of diversity and particularity, a 'new way of seeing'[6] which allows for unpredictability and intuition. Order isn't seen as a formal or theoretical problem, or as the imposition of abstract pattern on intractable matter. In studying the intricacies of apparently fickle behaviour, an alternative to the abstractions of theory is proposed, a series of interrelated systems of complexity which take their meaning from the irregularities of actual things. We may all be in some sense Amateur Scientists, with our own, individual grasp of a reality which is never fixed, but is in a state of perpetual change. This allows for the precision and the truth of subjectivity: a position which is neither naive nor retrogressive, but liberating.

CAROLINE COLLIER

1 see Roland Barthes *The Death of the Author*, in *Image-Music-Text*, Hill and Wang, New York, 1977

2 'Protegez-moi, Mon Seigneur

mon Navire est si petit et

Votre Mer est si grand.'

3 Gaston Bachelard *The Poetics of Space*, Beacon Press, Boston, 1969, pp XIII - XV

4 Marcel Proust *A Selection from the Miscellaneous Writings*, chosen and translated by Gerard Hopkins, Allan Wingate, London 1948

5 see Jean Baudrillard *Selected Writings* Polity Press, Cambridge, (in association with Basil Blackwell, Oxford), 1988 *Consumer Society* pp33-5

6 see James Gleick *Chaos: Making a New Science*, Sphere Books Ltd (Penguin) London 1988

The Artists

Lea Andrews

It's very important for me to understand why I make art in the way I do and to recognise and become fully conscious of the reasons behind its realisation.

When I consider the origins of *this* work I'm aware of a great mix of feelings and ideas and of a motivation which comes from a reservoir of experience, somewhere within me. There is a need to find expression for these experiences and to communicate with people but there is also a need to make images which, through their making, offer me the chance to understand and in a sense to 'become free' from these feelings and ideas. I don't see this as a denial of the work, its meaning or method, but simply as an aim, or a reason for making visual what is inexpressible in any other form. I feel there is more to be revealed to me and it's this process of revelation which fascinates me. I like not being totally in control of what I do. It's as reassuring as it can be frightening.

I've been returning to the place where I was born to make work for several years now and it's obvious to me that in going home I am trying to resolve feelings from my childhood I experienced there. This has become a great source for my work and my dreams from that time are just as important to me as any other memories I have of it. Making art there is a way of realising my attachment to the past and to the sense of belonging which has always been so crucial to me.

The village where I was born has little recorded history however, as it has grown slowly from nothing, over the past hundred years, upon what was once common land. I wanted to be able to invent a history for it by making photographic versions of 'false' public sculptures which inform its origins, its existence. In previous work I've made attempts to deal with a photographic interpretation of sculpture and I'd always been drawn to public art, and especially figurative sculpture. I also wanted to make some intervention that wasn't fixed in a gallery setting and to make work outside, for the appreciation or criticism of a public not often exposed to work like this.

There is a growing awareness that I want to make work which offers 'service' to people. I want my work to make people think about the world, about themselves, and the gap between us which is the only real hurdle we face. Making art is becoming my attempt at jumping that hurdle.

Lea Andrews, September, 1989

Maquette for 'Young Tom and old Dobbin discover Sonning Common' (Public sculpture, Private land) 1989
Colour cibachrome 121 x 152cm Courtesy the artist

Eric Bainbridge

In the past I would collect different kinds of object quickly, almost forcing them together and inventing parts. I would sometimes transfer a particular feature or detail from one thing to another. Now I am more selective and look for objects with particular qualities both abstract and referential. At the same time I interfere less with what I finally use.

What remains a constant quality in the objects I choose is an inexpressiveness, a dumbness, an ambiguity of identity. It's not important that they be instantly recognisable: even I don't know what some of them are. Generally of humble origin, they can either be fragments of a larger organisation of objects, or designed to be single ornaments. Sometimes they make their own reference to other sorts of art in the sense that everything around us that is designed is somehow styled in relation to art.

I am less interested in the sociological phenomenon of mass production than in its results. I often retain manufacturing information like moulding details or casting holes.

I try to look at these things in a way they haven't been looked at before. I'm not trying to explain anything other than our potential understanding of them. Which isn't to say I could ever simply re-present an object exactly as it is: that seems to me one of the more boring aspects of some recent sculpture. I need to play around with the size of the objects — increasing them to above human scale — and also to remake them myself, to remove them from their original world into the world of sculpture. I also began to use synthetic fur, about five years ago, as a way to disguise or camouflage something. Now I am more interested in how it is the most synthetic of products, precisely because it refers back so readily to our animal past. Otherwise, I make very utilitarian decisions about size or materials.

People may find abstract qualities in my work. I could never fully believe in the non-referentiality of minimal art, and was also more interested in what I read as its psychological side. No matter how unrecognisable an object I make, our desire to try and identify it is so strong. Minimalism was important for clearing away the accumulated rubbish from sculpture: it allowed us to start putting things back in. My art is inclusive rather than exclusive. Anything can go in as long as I find a way to order it.

I recognise that play is important. Physical or intellectual play is involved in anything that's created. But my sculptures are not toys, any more than they are replicas of real things. They are very consciously made as art. I'm not trying either to degrade high art or to elevate kitsch but maybe to do something in between, something different: to point to how the humblest things that we have created as a culture can have read in them, or projected into them, everything that we know about ourselves. They contain our potential, our extremes.

From a conversation with Eric Bainbridge, October, 1989

More Blancmange 1989
Plywood, plaster and fur fabric 228 x 276 x 58cm Courtesy Salvatore Ala Gallery, New York

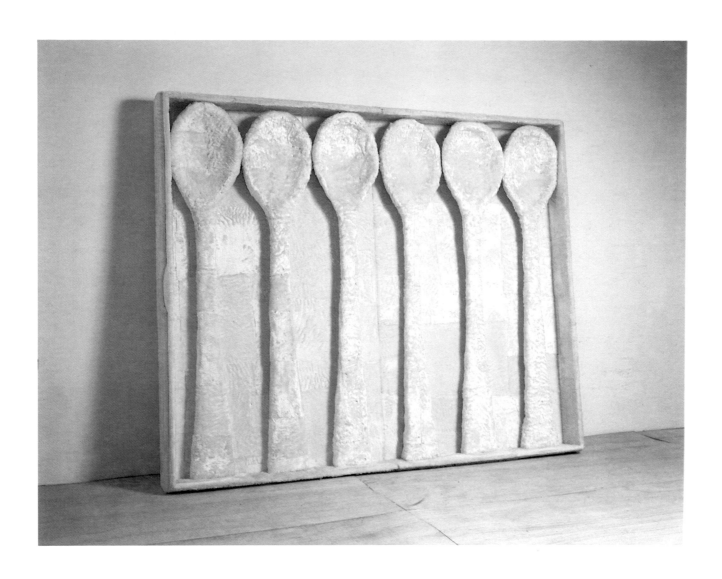

Black Audio Film Collective

Twilight City is a film about London at the end of the 1980s; a film about lost love and the end of an old London. In the story of that ending we have perhaps found another story; that of the voice of doubt/dissent and its slow erosion.

Twilight City is also about the loss of a sense of place, a sense of home. This is the London of flux and indeterminacy, the home of new doubts and newer losses. And beyond the grand narratives of geopolitical transformation and the forgrounding of the 'market' as the 'thing' which structures all human relations lies an old necessity: that of rescue and recuperation. *Twilight City* is about the business of counting our losses and refiguring our hopes.

The setting is a dark, decaying industrial centre, the scene of a search for love. In the course of the film this search for love becomes a search for the 'grain' of a sense of self; a quest for old maps of identity.

Twilight City is a tentative recuperation of that most minor moment into which an irreducible, inexchangable sense of self might be inscribed; the moment in which the story of the self is written as a litany of hope.

November 1989

Twilight City 1989
16mm film, colour 52min

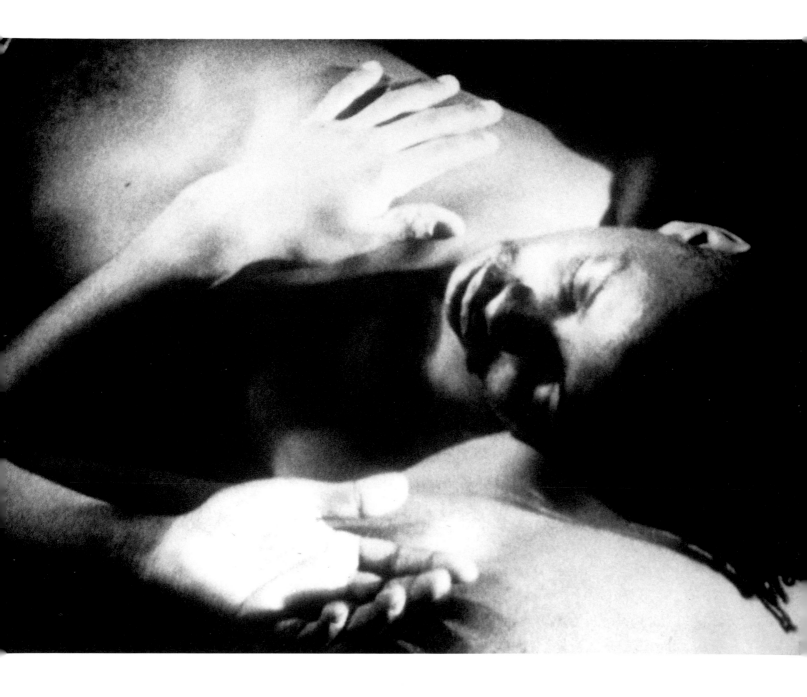

Sonia Boyce

He blushed each time they met in public.
    Tigger seeks Winnie the Pooh
    to share pots of honey
    and bouncing
All she wanted to know
Was it good for you?
Was it good for you? Too. Know she knew you.

Her eyes sparkled each time they met in public.
    Well heeled wild angel
    seeks
    creamy velvet underground
As she caressed. Her hand in hand. She wondered.
Would anyone know?

Colour photograph 1989
Colour photocopy 22.3 x 18.5cm Courtesy the artist

Jyll R. Bradley

URBAN COWBOYS
(for women who want the same)

In momentary crisis, the Western artist's yearning for revitalisation in the face of bankruptcy has become a 'pilgrimage' in search of lost utopias.[1] In this, the artist pauses before different shrines, from Otherness to Otherness: racial, cultural, sexual. S/he wanders between them in a perpetual 'act' of self-catharsis — replenishing, emptying, fulfilling, taking care never to leave her/his trace, disturb the 'primordial' scene or to pass too far from 'home'.

Because s/he cannot locate us, we are rendered unknown and thus at once marked: Honoured (in appropriate circles), Tremendously Desirable (in private confession), but above all feared.

For her/his 'cannot' has become the unspeakable Truth of her/his entire experiencing of us. In their new role as colonisers, they grow hard together adrift in this fabulous void, this intriguing abyss in which they are at once sure and afraid of/for themselves. They call names into their silence,

then they listen for echoes.
Each says: "I have projected myself into the Other with such power that when I am without the Other I cannot recover myself, regain myself: I am lost forever."[2]

In so doing, in a moment's abandonment s/he can thus enrich her/himself, make this impoverished self a touch more attractive, a little more polemical in moments of awkwardness whilst maintaining at all times an appearance of utmost control.

Jyll Bradley, October 1989
1) See Jean Fisher, 'Other Cartographies', in *Third Text* no. 6, p.79
2) *A Lover's Discourse*, Roland Barthes, trans. Richard Howard (London, Jonathan Cape, 1979).

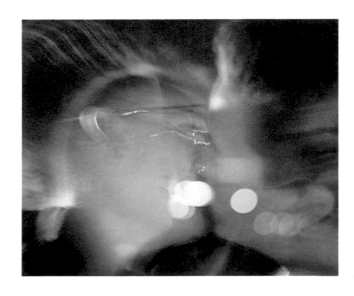

Kate Bright

Landscape has always been my touchstone. I'm particularly interested in the structure of things and investigations into physics and geology seem natural to me. Acquiring the knowledge is important: a way of explaining the world that is not aesthetic but is factual and unromantic.

The work exhibited is from a series of paintings derived from the Yugoslavian landscape. I don't paint a scene because I want to catch the colour of the light on the stone and the dew on the grass. The paintings represent drystone walls: a way that man draws on the landscape, evidence of our presence and manipulation of the land. For me there is an interest in the simultaneous existence of the natural and the man-made within the landscape.

From a conversation with Kate Bright, October 1989

Untitled 1988
Oil and pigment on canvas 167 x 152cm Courtesy the artist

Melanie Counsell ✳✳

'Humanistic' is a word that I have associated with my concerns as an artist over the last year. It seems fitting because it is wide-ranging, including social and psychological implications that I feel are present in the work.

The work is mainly site specific installation. For me, this means attempting to create a full collaboration between a space and the atmosphere of that environment and the concerns I am dealing with. Rather than imposing into a space I think it is more appropriate to look for 'clues' — architecturally and atmospherically — to form the basis of how the work might look within the space. This should result in a work that has the appearance of belonging in a space or that it has always existed there.

I have attempted recently to deal with aspects of grief, melancholy, human tragedy or loss. The initial intention is to produce a piece that could be somewhat disturbing or unsettling to the spectator.

A recurring element has been the use of water, flowing, dripping, seeping or still. Our need for water is obvious, indeed it is the basis for all life. But water has also become a symbol of pollution and threat to health. It implies both life and death. In two works the use of water has directly related to the act of crying. Barthes describes weeping in terms of the liquid expansion of our own bodies . . . and the 'truest' of messages from the body . . .

Melanie Counsell, October 1989

In this show: Untitled 1990
12 filing cabinets
12 rolled carpets —
and water

bottom drawer of cabinet open (½) filled w. water w roll of old floral carpet inside.

Installation at Matt's Gallery, November 1989
White tiles, carpet, water, chintz curtain and copper pipes

Matthew Dalziel

Unseen, Unheard but Measured is my third work to date concerned with the consequences of human work and production. The production processes of a society not only reflect but also influence its attitudes. At the heart of a system of work lies a system of values and, more precisely, a view of the individual's relationship with others and his reason for existence.

Unseen, Unheard but Measured was made at Shell UK Exploration and Productions Gas Plant at St Fergus, on the north east coast of Scotland. This is one of the few high security industrialised plants in Britain. It is also one of the most technologically advanced in the world. The work is an installation consisting of ten large-scale radiographic images of welds, and two video monitors which relay images and information concerning the location of the plant, with a time lapse of fourteen years.

I recognised that within the imagery and physicality of the radiographs existed many of the qualities that were central to the subject I was coming to terms with. The radiographs were produced in different countries, demonstrating the ability of multi-national companies to transcend national frontiers. Each image reveals a discontinuity or, in less technical language, a flaw, which implies a potential danger. The abstract and linear energy of the radiographs expresses an activity which is intrinsic to some forms of physics — that when an energy is put into motion it travels in one direction only. I believe western civilisation in a sense to be like this: abstract forces far beyond human scale or control have emerged through time, engulfing traditional ways of life and indigenous cultures in an unstoppable progression towards a singular end. Computer-aided technology is adding to this momentum at a frightening rate.

In the two videos we can see an example of how rapid this change actually is. In fourteen years an area of land and a way of life which supported a farmer and his family have been transformed into a futuristic, highly complex industrial plant.

With this work I hope to encourage people to consider and evaluate the changes taking place in our society. We are caught up in a way of life which is seldom questioned and there is a tendency to think of all progress as 'good', never giving a thought to what it has supplanted. Those of us who do stop to think may feel helpless to change things.

The little video of Pittenheath Farm strengthens my faith, optimism, and hope. The young man who made the film quite naturally and unselfconsciously directs all his attention to the things of real value in his life — his animals, his home and the people he loves.

Installation made during a four month residency, initiated and funded by the Scottish Arts Council, at Shell UK Exploration and Productions Gas Plant, St Fergus.

Still images, monitors 1 and 2 from **Unseen, Unheard but Measured**, 1989.

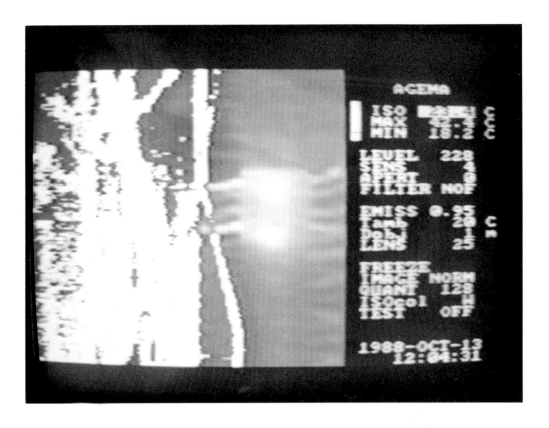

Ian Davenport

Notes on Painting:

I use household and industrial paints, the fluidity of the material and the quantity I can obtain excite me.

I dip a brush in a paint pot and then with a fully laden brush make contact with the canvas.

The rhythm of the painting comes from repetition — a kind of exuberant methodicalism.

The paintings are a whole — what happens in one section will reoccur in another.

Chance within a highly structured system.

My paintings always surprise me, no matter how clear they are to me from the outset.

Each painting has a plan: this might change during its execution and often the painting is the result of many plans.

The structure of the painting is formed by the paint running into itself. Each of my paintings has evolved from a very deliberate process, not from intuitive mark-making.

I always try to do very little but a lot of it.

I don't say this painting looks like this or that, the whole painting might be about something, more likely a phenomenon than an object. But the meaning comes from the making of the painting.

The realisation of ideas formulates taste. My work necessitates the questioning of good taste.

Ian Davenport, September 1989

Untitled 1989
Oil on canvas 214 x 213cm Courtesy Waddington Galleries, London

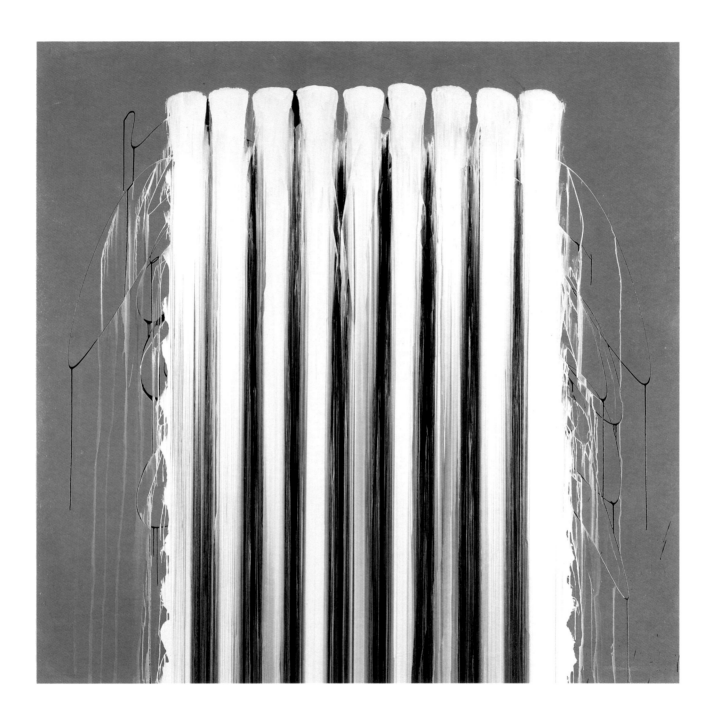

Grenville Davey ✳

One or other . . .

There is a way in which you can describe each partner in *Right 3rd and 6th* as 'unique' but infectious. It cannot be taken as read that a desire to reconcile them as a pair is wholly 'natural', or that there is a central goal or shared point of origin. They were never at any imaginary moment unified nor is their inertness a result of their separation or isolation. Each one is unique in that its potential is disproportionately set . . . and that . . . one or other at any point becomes the discrete partner suggests that to resolve them as a whole is somehow expected.

The only thing the two parts have in common is that they were cut from the same piece of material; but from then on they were developed independently.

In some of the earlier pieces, I used nuts and bolts often in a decorative manner and I have made works that were theatrical enough to imply a rhythm, an activity, outside themselves. References were usually to man-made things. In *Right 3rd and 6th* it is clear that there is a reference and that it is to something organic: they feel they are made of something which is likely to alter its state. But the references are left inert, they are almost not there.

From a conversation with Grenville Davey, November 1989

Right 3rd and 6th 1989
Painted steel and hardboard diameter 152.5 x 62cm each Courtesy Dakis Joannou, Athens

Cathy de Monchaux

. . . the work is the result of a build up of details, which are the invented solutions to the problems posed when you try to attach things to each other which aren't normally attached . . .

. . . the work resolves itself when every part is accounted for . . . put in its place . . .

. . . when the objects work, it seems almost quite natural for them to be as they are, although on closer inspection I think they frustrate because they deny the expectation that they will function in some way . . . Hopefully the relationship with the viewer is one of unconsummatable flirtation and desire . . .

. . . for me the interest lies in making it look charged . . . something that you can engage with because it seems to be put there for a reason . . . ultimately the reason refers back to the object . . .

From a conversation with Cathy de Monchaux, September 1989

Secrete 1989
Aluminium, velvet, zips 22 x 220 x 12cm Private Collection

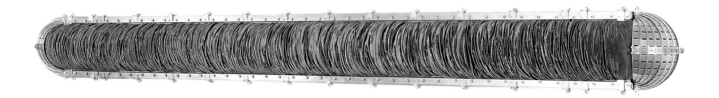

Locky Morris ⚹

The pieces that are being shown oppose partition, normalisation policies and neo-colonialism. They oppose British and all cultures of repression. Britain's domination over Ireland for 800 years was achieved by the systematic dismantling of its culture.

This is not British Art. It is Irish Art from the North of Ireland. It should be seen as a small but proud contribution towards a culture of self determination and democracy in Ireland.

In the period from 1971 to 1986, the security forces searched 338,803 houses, some 75 per cent of all houses in Northern Ireland. Again, as the vast majority of the house searches were in Catholic areas it is more realistic to relate the figures to the 170,000 Catholic dwellings in Northern Ireland. This suggests that the total number of searches is the equivalent of searching every Catholic home on two occasions. Many homes would not be under suspicion so it is reasonable to conclude that certain homes would have been searched perhaps as many as ten or more times.

Justice Under Fire
The abuse of Civil Liberties in Northern Ireland
Edited by Anthony Jennings LL.B., Pluto Press, 1988.

Locky Morris was born in Derry in 1960 where he continues to live and work. He doesn't work as an isolated individual but in collaboration with the collective experience and history of his community. His sculptures represent the experience and hopes of Derry people living in the most militarized zone in Western Europe.

Is sinne pobal na streachailte
Claochlaionn an cultúr s'againne

Locky Morris, November 1989

View of Dawn Raid
Pilots Row Centre, Rossville Street, Bogside, Derry Cardboard, masking tape, paint

Jeffrey Dennis

Stories are the way we learn about the world. I am not sure, despite the proverb, that it is possible for a picture to tell a story. But they may be 'carriers': just as, at any point in a tale, you, the listener, must keep hold of all the threads running away from that point, back and forth in time; I try to make these physical objects hold the chromosome of a narrative.

A painting, to have any kind of autonomy, must convince the viewer that it presents a painted world with its own natural forces and obligations; different, possibly, but as inescapable as gravity is to us. However, it is possible for that world to have many points of transaction with our own. The need to make a resemblance is fundamental.

Images from photography and film find their reflection in my pictures as the 'touch-plates' of extended senses, by which we try to know or feel things (and I do not despair that we can really do that). But they are only one particular currency of truth.

Scientists and thinkers, to make an idea concrete and graspable by the imagination, build a model. This may serve, with additions and adjustments, until some irrepressible fact or notion emerges which is incompatible. The model must then be toppled and begun again. This way of working appeals to me; adding to a structure until it is pushed to the point of dissolution.

I would like to make a new kind of Pre-Raphaelite painting; but not in a revivalist or nostalgic sense. I respond to the fictional space, the shifting realism found in the work of Medieval artists. Informal, expedient, and full of resourceful dualities, they conduct a sort of wrestling match with a flat tapestry to pull from it an illusion of a field or cell. The patterning re-weaves lost links between the visual sense and those of sound, smell, taste and touch.

There is a powerful imaginative motor that cuts in when the idle gaze is held by wallpaper, by a screed of cement, by the little piece of infinity offered by a picture on a can of peas: this is my kind of landscape: a sounding board or screen, or, rubbed through, an escape hatch.

The characters in my paintings are colonists in this difficult terrain. They bring all sorts of awkward luggage and allegiances from their previous homes, and stake out new territory.

Jeffrey Dennis, September 1989

Heartwood 1989
Oil on canvas 228 x 213cm Courtesy Salvatore Ala Gallery, New York

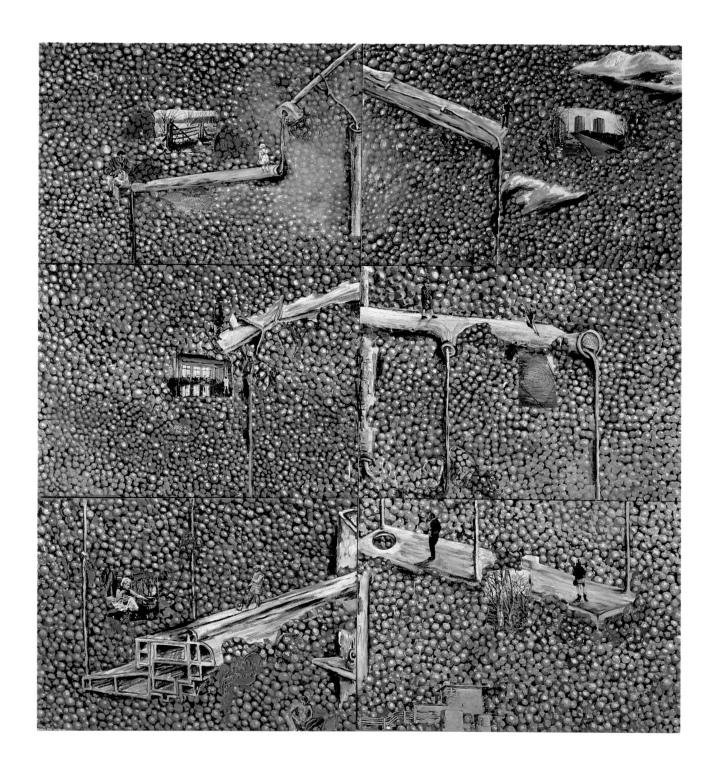

Willie Doherty

Although my works are about specific places and ideas I think the meaning broadens out. Northern Ireland is still a testing ground and the kind of planning that goes on there can be seen as part of a larger policy of organisation and control that will probably become more common in British cities over the next few years. Surveillance, for instance, is an issue that people in lots of places have become much more aware of, because their personal privacy has been increasingly encroached upon.

More recently the work has become involved with notions of identity, or maybe even nationality and how those ideas are constructed. For example, in the event of a bombing incident in Britain the usual stereotypes of the Irish as inherently violent, stupid etc. are brought into force and, since discussions about Ireland are either silenced or removed from any social or political context, the response is one of outrage and bewilderment. This work attempts to relocate or bring back on the agenda some of those social, political and economic factors which are pertinent to understanding the colonial relationship between Britain and Ireland.

My use of language is different in the recent Belfast work. Words like 'Isolate' and 'Sever' seem more imposed on the landscape, so that there is the idea of the language not being from there but imposed like a policy or strategy. They are also more direct: with just one word, you are forced to make a more literal connection between the image and the word. This is very different in tone from some of the work in Derry, which was more about using a language coming from that situation, more organic.

It is important that the work operates outside of the marginalised context where it comes from. It's useful that it is located within the art world and can intervene in galleries and exhibitions such as this one, and become part of a process of unearthing ideas that are off the agenda in Britain.

From a conversation with Willie Doherty, October 1989

Strategy, The Westlink, West Belfast, 1989
photograph with text 121 x 182cm each Courtesy the artist

Mona Hatoum ✳✳

THE LIGHT AT THE END

In the process of developing a piece of work, I go through a rigorous paring down of all that is superfluous to arrive at a precise and contained form. Always in my work in all its manifestations, whether it is performance, video or installation work, formal considerations are of primary importance.

In *The light at the end* I adopt a 'minimal' aesthetic, but unlike minimal sculpture, the piece is referential and reverberates with meaning and associations. The theme of a divide, a psychic and physical barrier has been central to my work, often referring to social, political and historical divisions. This is partly a personal metaphor but I think my most successful work has managed to distance itself from any personal or historical specificities.

My work is often strongly paradoxical. The title *The light at the end* sets up an expectation of optimism which is then disrupted when the work is experienced physically. Violence and danger are not just inferred but are actually present within the work, to set up in the viewer conflicting emotions of attraction and repulsion, desire and revulsion.

From a conversation with Mona Hatoum, October, 1989

The light at the end 1989
Angle iron metal frame and 6 electric elements

Kevin Henderson

My works are organisations of images. I don't see them as sculptural. I use discarded materials and recurring motifs instead of dense imagery, simple organisation rather than elaborate composition.

I like to feel that I can work with any material. I'm not biased towards any one thing but if I moved from where I am living now, then the materials I use would undoubtedly change. I usually choose something that someone else has used before or that has served some other purpose. What matters to me is not so much that things have been made by somebody as that they have been used by somebody.

Ideas or concepts, regardless of importance, are similarly only materials. They are there to be used – like images, or the things the works are assembled from, they are intrinsic to the construction of meaning.

For me meaning can be determined by understanding use and not just by an act of recognition.

Our media traffics in images that create and are created by a visual culture that at best can be described as perverse. It relentlessly demands obedience.

In contemporary understanding of progress, a change of direction, a discovery, marks a different (and by implication a better) stage. Seeing progress this way is readily accepted because it is no more than empty change. It devalues the achievements of the past.

In my work the past is inherent in the material itself. Time is present, as an entity and as a theme. *Propaganda Cradle* has 89 repetitions of a single motif – an altered emblem from a perpetual calendar in a 12th-century Ottoman manuscript.

Kevin Henderson, October 1989

Propaganda Cradle 1989
Wood and oil paint 15 x 245 x 520cm Courtesy the artist

Gary Hume

The paintings are not abstract or monochromatic. I'm painting paintings of <u>doors</u> in one colour, sanding and painting, sanding and painting in gloss, which is impenetrable, domestic stuff. The paintings are beautiful but blunt.

I see them as unheroic. There is no essential core of meaning but they are meaningful through cognition and in their relation to the synchronic state of art and society, whilst they remain an empty sign, a door motif in a potentially endless series — simultaneously spacious and oppressive.

From a conversation with Gary Hume, September 1989

Magnolia 1989
Gloss paint on canvas 254 x 162cm Courtesy Karsten Schubert Ltd, London

Kabir Hussain

My work covers four areas: installations, large sculpture related to the human scale, small bronzes and photography. The installations are central to my concept of sculpture. The essence of these works lies in their physical relationship to an individual. The large-scale nature of the installations and the way that they occupy a space allow a person to participate and explore the work in a more direct way than is normally possible with sculpture. Similarly, with the small bronze landscapes the participant travels through the vast landscape via the imagination.

The concept of the 'universal' fascinates me. The aim in my work is to concern myself primarily with a 'global' landscape. This is inspired by my desire during my childhood to visit different continents. The sculptures seek to convey connotations of 'far away places'.

The bronze landscapes were brought into realisation after a three month study visit to Peru in 1986. The pieces are a direct response to the Peruvian landscape. Scale is of utmost importance. The works contradict their size — they aspire to fulfil their potential to evoke an all-embracing environment. The pieces are a reflection of my experience of being within that landscape. In *Sullstani* the impeccably flat altiplano leads the eye into an unending distance: almost within arm's reach the sky levels out above one's head.

Kabir Hussain, September 1989

Sullstani 1989
Bronze 1 x 5 x 17cm Courtesy the artist (illustrated actual size)

Bethan Huws **

Show contained c. 14 of these little "boats" — grouped in 4 cases....

A natural line turns on herself.

A fragment of natural anxiety.

An emotional aloneness.

A conversation on ephemeral fragility.

Untitled 1983-
An assembled rush 30mm in length Courtesy the artist (Illustrated actual size)

Callum Innes

I want to present something which exists in its own right, and these works are attempts to embody and reflect natural processes.

In the initial stages, the organisation of the marks is deliberate and controlled. I create a vocabulary of marks. These quotations have their own intrinsic qualities and histories. They then assume their independence through the reaction of paint and turpentine.

I let the paint react across the surface of the canvas or paper, allowing turpentine to drop down in verticals. I determine what is going to happen, yet the picture changes in the making. The way that the turpentine spreads depends on how much I add, and how quickly. Painting is usually additive: my paintings are built up and erased. They often appear to have an essential frailty.

When a painting is done, I don't feel that my personality is hanging on the wall, for all to see. It is a piece of work that I have organised and then presented.

From a conversation with Callum Innes, September 1989

Cento I 1989
Oil and turpentine on oil paper 200 x 100cm Courtesy the artist

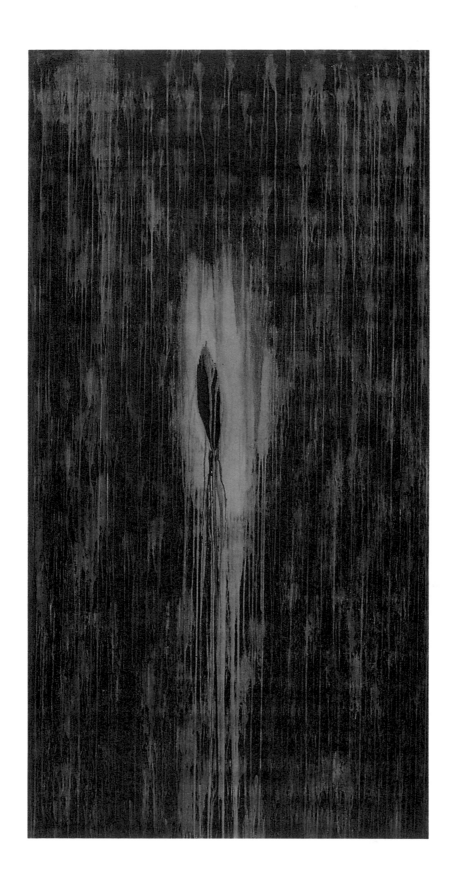

Brian Jenkins

My work is made as an exploration of defiance,
creating difficulties and obstacles which I strive to
overcome.

Through using photography, performance,
installation, drawing and super 8 film, I try to explore
questions of space and environment which are not
normally associated with and are sometimes denied to
someone with a physical handicap such as my own. For
myself, working within these extremely difficult and
demanding areas and environments helps create a
platform for exorcising taboos and prejudice associated
with being physically handicapped.

There are particular barriers which are set up in
landscapes which are massive to me . . . fences,
ditches, rough terrain, paths . . . and this kind of need
builds up . . . you want something so much but you
can't actually get it and you try to make something
visible by making a piece of art. I hope my work allows
a challenge to preconceived ideas and attitudes.

The work in the show forms a self-portrait,
consisting of an installation drawing relating to
photographic images of a particular landscape.

Brian Jenkins, September 1989

*outside installation of
outline of figure
drawn w. limestone(?)
rocks — same red —
looked like self-inflicted
wound ....*

Elevation II 1989 *not the one*
Courtesy the artist *in show*

Patrick Keiller

VALTOS is the film of a chase. It was one of ten films and videotapes made very quickly as the second stage of an open competition to produce four works for the television series *Ghosts in the Machine*. The plan was that the ten would be made as 'pilots', and then four of them would be made *again* for television.

In fact VALTOS was transmitted without this duplication, but the idea that we* were chasing the film, and that the film was chasing its double, was the only element of narrative that we set out with, apart from the itinerary.

I have made several films from journeys, writing the story only after editing the picture, but I had never made one in Britain before. I chose VALTOS as the destination because it is a long way away (it is on the west coast of the Isle of Lewis). I had had it in mind since a previous visit. The idea of the headlong northward chase is borrowed from *Frankenstein*, and the *double* is a Scots motif in, for example, James Hogg's . . . *Confessions of a Justified Sinner*. VALTOS also sounds a bit like VATHEK.

The film is an attempt at *genre* The idea was to combine these 'supernatural' elements with a landscape tradition, of, say, Edwin Smith (in the *Shell Guides*), *Night Mail* or *Listen to Britain*, and make something new and strange.

Most of the preoccupations of the film are derived from its rudimentary form. The disembodied voice and camera, wandering in the landscape, lead to a 'mechanical' approximation of altered consciousness and hence to Frankenstein and the supernatural. The *grain* of the film and the deliberate cultivation of indeterminacy and weather lead to Brownian motion, turbulence, and simple-minded attempts to imagine the *molecular* basis of consciousness, and of history in the landscape.

The real origin of the film, though, (and of the others), is in 'a profane illumination, a materialistic, anthropological inspiration' (Walter Benjamin) — the surrealist *frisson* of place, that is so carefully identified in Louis Aragon's *Le Paysan de Paris*.

Patrick Keiller, November, 1989
*ie Julie Norris and myself

VALTOS or The Veil
Camera Patrick Keiller & Julie Norris
Text Patrick Keiller
Voice Vladek Sheybal
Commissioned by the Arts Council of Great Britain, Channel Four Television and Illuminations
Distributed by the London Film Makers' Co-op

Valtos or **The Veil** 1987
16mm black and white film 11 minutes

Joanna Kirk ✳

Clothes w. personality left

Pastel is a very immediate, direct, medium. Everything is built up until it has a precise look. I want the pictures to be well-drawn, highly finished, to be decorative, full of pattern, delicate. The content should remain enigmatic. The last thing I want is to make expressive pastel drawings. I want them to be tight. The gesture is in the way the picture is arranged.

I always work from photographs. It's important to me that people get the sense of a missing original. The background colour is always apparent in the source image — if the background isn't right the fragments don't work. Often the gaps speak about my interpretation of the source photograph: what I leave out matters.

I'm interested in show, pomp, order and finery, in all kinds of arrangements and artifice and propriety. I like drawing materials, flowers, feathers. I'm attracted to glinting things. The drawings are arrangements on the paper.

The source for *Cardinals* consisted of a photograph of rows of cardinals in full regalia. I was attracted by the richness and the overt decoration, by the Catholicism, of an image which at the same time appeared authoritarian. All I wanted to show was the lace, the most decorative part of the picture. Clearly each bit of lace, with its symbolic design, is inhabited, structured — it is part of someone. The picture ended up as being four portraits of absent people — individual bits of lace. The image flows so your eyes read from one to the next like an animated cartoon. You don't quite know what you're looking at. For me it's an intense image — yet it was only a tiny bit of the original picture, torn from a magazine.

From a conversation with Joanna Kirk, October, 1989

✳ **Cardinals** 1989
Pastel on paper 127 x 91.4cm (x4 parts) Courtesy the Contemporary Art Society

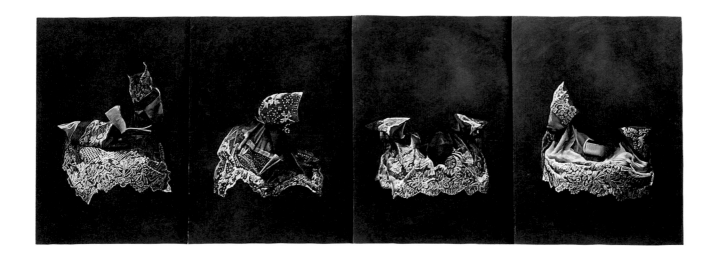

Elizabeth Magill

Any single interpretation negates others that are possible, and it is the endless possibilities that I enjoy. Sometimes I repeat stencils of cars because there are lots of cars. I like to construct an overall view and then particularise it.

Colour coding and numbering give a notional identity to things that appear random or similar. They are a way of imposing an immediate recognisable order. The process makes finite the numerically inconceivable, locating, labelling and controlling, it comes down to a desire to understand.

Elizabeth Magill, November 1989

Fish and Fleur de Lys 1989
Oil on canvas 213 x 183cm Courtesy Dieter Bergman, Dublin

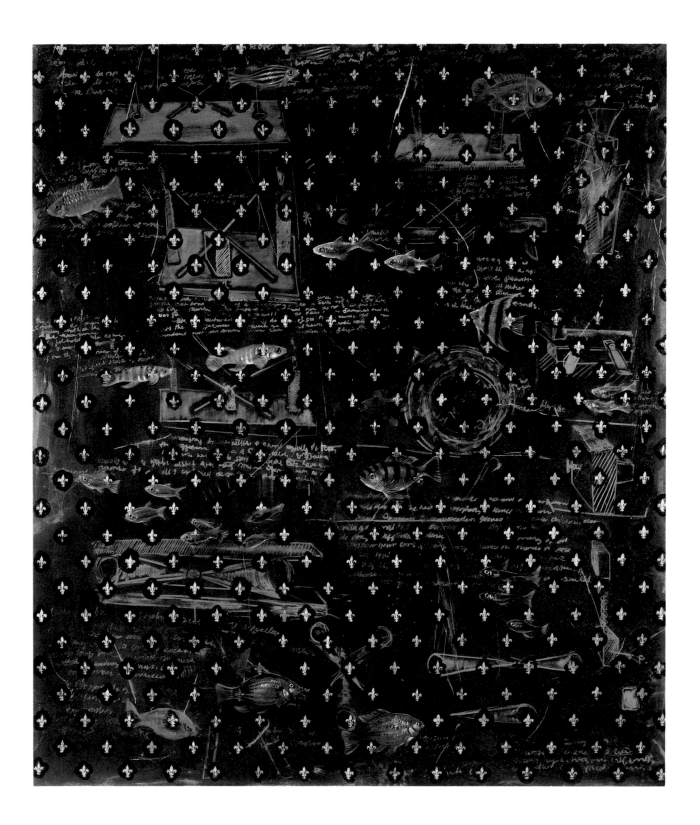

Lisa Milroy

From a conversation with David Ward November 1989

D.W.: Can we talk about the distribution, organisation, ordering and positioning in the paintings possibly having significance over the objects depicted because your repertoire of subjects hasn't expanded indefinitely.

L.M.: For the moment I seem to have settled on a range of objects that fall into a definite number of groups. The tyres, stamps, lightbulbs, shoes, Greek vases, hardware . . . they interest me both as objects — what they look like and what they suggest — and how they can act as the building blocks of painting. The objects may stay the same from painting to painting but their ordering suggests different sets of ideas. In one painting lightbulbs were arranged along the lines of a broken grid, some concentrated in evenly organized groups, others travelling in horizontal or vertical lines, leading the eye up and down and from side to side across the canvas. I thought that the composition suggested the pattern of what city blocks and streets can look like, seen from above — or, on a micro-scale, the pattern that those small gadgets make on the panels inside transister radios. Lightbulbs, with associations of conducting energy, of communities, and of light itself, seemed like good objects to use in this way to talk about these things.

D.W.: What about this lightbulb painting? The distribution here is different — analogous to constellations . . .

L.M.: The ordering in this painting is much more random. I've been looking at space photographs for some time now — how the photograph makes a black square on the page, and the stars within it a seemingly random pattern of white, heavily clustered in some areas, in specks and dispersed trails in others . . . but I think it's more the overall pattern I'm responding to than the stars themselves. When I paint objects, I try to sum them up in a way connected to the idea I have of them, treat them as if they were generic . . . It's interesting to think of certain patterns or orders as being generic as well.

Another photograph comes to mind of a beach scene, where people have arrived and put themselves down all over the place according to no particular plan

Lightbulbs 1989 *badly realistic*
oil on canvas 203.2 x 259cm Courtesy Nicola Jacobs Gallery, London

— yet I read the image as a coherent one, almost as if recognising a certain kind of order, responding again not so much to the individuals but their distribution as clusters, dots and wavery lines, dark against the lighter tone of the beach, like the constellations in reverse. Lightbulbs in this painting echo such patterns.

J.W.: The painterly engagement you have when you are making the work means that every mark is a particular decision to do with distribution.

L.M.: Yes — I'm aware of the lightbulbs as conductors of certain associations, but I'm also conscious of how they can be depicted in paint, as a series of marks and colours — a dynamic builds up in the placing of the lightbulbs as groups of different sizes of marks here and there across the canvas, so that although I am thinking outside the painting to patterns such as the ones we've been talking about, the painting generates its own logic about where things should go, and is self-contained. . .

D.W.: There is again that perception of order becoming the subject, rather than, say, finding a way of depicting an object. How do you compare the random ordering in the paintings of stamps and shoes with the lightbulbs?

L.M.: They all have distinct associations — yet it seems reasonable in my mind to place all three groups of objects on canvases in ways that are not totally dissimilar to one another. These paintings can be described as congregations of objects separated by large or small tracts of white ground. Yet similar patterns or compositions seem to accommodate specific associations and ideas triggered by each individual set of objects. In terms of, say, the shoes I wondered what kind of image might result from the passage of people hurrying down a side-walk freezing for a split second, — the constant motion being a rapid series of individual still moments, like frames in a film. Stamps bring to my mind notions of travel, picturing in miniature different aspects of the world. The stamps are so small in relation to the huge size of the canvas that my eye feels as though it has to travel a great distance to look from a community of stamps on one side of the painting, to another on the other side. Compass readings of north, south, east and west, replace more conventional orientations of left, right, up and down. And as for the lightbulbs, I think maybe I've said enough about them for the time being . . .

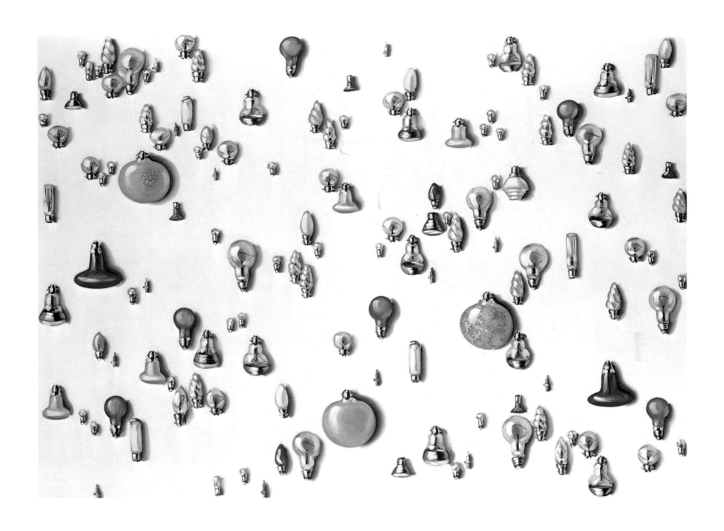

John Mitchell

The 'use value' of the bulk of the materials and objects incorporated in this current work has expired. The elements in each arrangement — cardboard boxes, wooden boxes, sections of billboard posters, metal grills etc — are either sought out or found by chance and 'salvaged'.

By collecting, selecting, editing and combining it is intended that new 'meanings' occur. The transformation of the original functions of language and materials has the potential to subvert accepted understandings, interpretations and associations.

Titles arise from, and are suggested by, symbols, handling instructions and places of origin marked on the boxes as well as by the type and nature of the materials and object used. When brought together these create a degree of tension necessary for the occurrence of potential 'meaning' within the viewer's response.

John Mitchell, September 1989

Shipping the Rain Forest 1989
Billboard poster and wooden boxes 101 x 215cm Courtesy the artist

Julian Opie

From a conversation with David Ward November 1989

D.W. This work has a relationship to corridors and screened partition areas found for example in airport architecture, transit point architecture . . In those sorts of interiors there are spaces divided in functional ways, but those functional intentions have a visual effect so that when we are walking through them we are in spaces which open up into transparencies, that reveal themselves through distance . . .

J.O. Yes, but I don't think their design is as unselfconscious as that, I think the designers of those places know what they are setting up visually — you are being dealt with in a very particular way for many reasons, one small one would be aesthetic — not so small — I think there is a kind of fantasy going on that is not recognised — if you look at 30s railway stations they are very different in design from Frankfurt airport although one would have thought both were just functional . . .

D.W. Is there some way in which the rows of dots that appear on the glass screens are an aestheticising of the kind of safety discs that appear on glass screens in airports and foyers?

J.O. I'm not sure but in a certain sense they are. I don't want to allow aestheticising to become something you absolutely don't want to get involved in, there is something very interesting about one's ability to aestheticise.

D.W. So, if you like, part of the function of the piece is an aesthetic function. Whereas the elements themselves are ordinary and utilitarian, it's how they engage with each other which is aesthetic.

J.O. Yes. This lends one back to being able to place the object. If one can place it entirely as an aesthetic object there is a way in which that defuses the object and makes it safe, however outrageous, that's OK because it can be put down to being aesthetic, whereas with what I am trying to do there is always another possibility, another argument. I don't think that many people would be convinced intellectually that one has actually wandered into the wrong place, that perhaps you should be going in here to get a form. What I find interesting is that if there is something in a white room

then it being art is very much one of the possibilities. There are a lot of fantastic things where you have to say "OK, I happen to be in a gallery, it happens to be a Tuesday, there is a guard looking at me but this is a Mondrian". What I want to do, and perhaps what Mondrian did at the same time, is to deal with everything . . . the white room, the guard and all the things that the work reminds you of . . .

D.W. The viewer's relationship to this work is not passive, to see it is literally to take part in it . . .

J.O. I think you should just look, don't think "is this good or is this bad?" and if in the process of seeing what you are seeing, which is not a difficult thing, things come up that interest you, you naturally stay around and then you move on. This movement is an aspect of this work, it's a way for me to deal with my own sense that when you present someone with something it is a kind of deadened situation. You look at it, it looks at you, nothing happens. It's not like a movie, so in a sense I am trying to find some diversion from that static situation. You have got to move to comprehend it even at the most basic level, just to figure out how to get round it you have got to move and to move you have got to look out where you are moving. You might be drawn into thinking what this thing is doing here. And the motive for that interest is that it looks good and therefore you are drawn to something that looks good, and then you want to know why and in the figuring out you have engaged with it . . .

D.W. Here it is very clear that in actual and direct ways you have set up something in which things can happen, but it is not your job to tell people what those things are going to be.

J.O. In order for that to function there are a lot of careful 'not doings'. To make something random you have to work hard to avoid patterns building up or avoid implications that you don't want. To allow the work to remain open means avoiding 'meaning' or a conclusion.

Construction 1989
Glass, Aluminium, Paint 188 x 324 x 405cm Courtesy Lisson Gallery

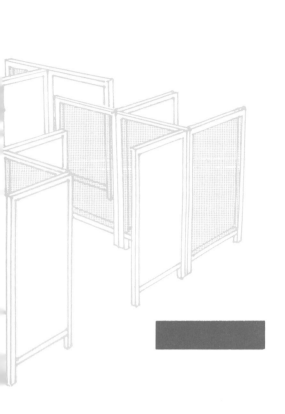

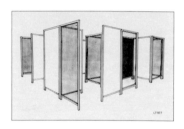

Cornelia Parker ✳

I've never made a solid grounded sculpture; I am more interested in the space within and around the mass, in atmosphere, in anti-matter. It is as if I am trying to make things vaporous so I can breathe them in and then exhale.

I have a collecting and cataloguing instinct, nurtured in childhood years spent on a smallholding. Every spare hour was filled with repetitive tasks: milking cows by hand, planting seeds in endless rows, picking, pruning or stringing up tomatoes. I feel as if the choreography hasn't changed, but now I use it to explore matter and what it means through sculpture.

I have a collection of children's encyclopaedias from the 1930s. They always use familiar buildings like the Empire State or St. Paul's as measures of scale, placed beside Everest or at the bottom of the deepest ocean. Gradually on my travels I was picking up souvenirs, crude representations of famous monuments. You buy this little cypher of a landmark and everyone knows you've been there, it's a token of an experience. When I began to use lead casts of these objects in my work, I was trying to describe a very intense experience which I found hard, the souvenirs for me were a starting point. You are using something visible that everyone recognises to describe the indescribable — taking something you know to explore the things you don't.

When I first started to hang objects from the ceiling, I was thinking about plumblines as evidence of gravity, and as instruments for devining. I like the idea of the pendulum as a measure of the unknown, what we can't see, what's beneath the earth. The plumbline points to a kind of underworld — dowsing the subterranean, subconscious areas of ourselves.

I was inspired by the way Gaudi worked out the plans for his buildings by hanging lead weights, wires and canvas from the ceiling, creating potential forms in space, then inverting them to make a structure that would defy gravity by standing up.

The silver objects in *Thirty Pieces of Silver* are very familiar; trophies, teapots, cigarette cases, spoons, candlesticks . . . Silver is commemorative, the objects are landmarks in people's lives. I wanted to change their meaning, their visibility, their worth, that is why I flattened them, consigning them all to the same fate. As a child I used to crush coins on a railway track — you couldn't spend your pocket money afterwards but you kept the metal slivers for their own sake, as an imaginative currency and as physical proof of the destructive powers of the world. I find the pieces of silver have much more *potential* when their meaning as everyday objects has been eroded. *Thirty Pieces of Silver* is about materiality and then about anti-matter. In the gallery the ruined objects are ghostly, levitating just above the floor, waiting to be re-assessed in the light of their transformation. The title, because of its biblical references, alludes to money, to betrayal, to death and resurrection: more simply it is a literal description of the piece.

From a conversation with Cornelia Parker, September 1989

Thirty Pieces of Silver 1988
Installation at Aspex Gallery, Portsmouth, May 1989 Crushed silver plate suspended on wire

Vongphrachanh Phaophanit

It began with a few family photographs, nothing could be more ordinary, more personal. These snap-shots were sent to me with letters during the last eighteen years. This is the only form of communication I have with my family in Laos. Eighteen years separate us, still these photographs and letters speak of people, places and lives of which I was formerly a part.

At first glance these images initiate a game of recognition; recognise her look, his clothes, someone's way of standing, another's hands . . . recognise those familiar details which time and distance have tried to abolish. The space which surrounds these photographs is imbued with an awareness of the *existence* of this past. In this way the effect these photographs have on me is as certain as that of memory, each one of them contains a fragment of the past.

Nothing but a moment of the past? Much more perhaps; something which being common to the past and present, is more essential than both —

Marcel Proust

The work deals with a few of these snap-shots and their effect at the present time. It intends neither to be autobiographical nor a nostalgic search for a childhood and an absent family. It is not an attempt to relate this story nor to present it in the form of a continuum. It starts rather at this point: that despite everything these images still create other meanings and that through these photographs a place exists which cannot be defined, reduced by language, where meanings are not fixed and identities not stable.

I wanted to explore memory through photographs, not in the way that we are taught to look at and take photographs — as 'compositions', as wholes. Looking at these snap-shots I began to realise that my eyes always wandered beyond the photograph as a whole in the search for details: a hand, an element of the background, a piece of clothing — supposedly 'insignificant' details but which held my attention. And then it was no longer a question of recognition but rather of fascination and it is this fascination that triggered off the work. I wanted to reproduce in images the way in which my eyes scoured these photographs — a gaze which was always searching for something, someone but which never took in the totality of the image.

In this sense the gaze is a memory in itself, constantly deferring from one detail to the next and never settling on a fixed whole; and memory, as seen in this piece, is made up of particles, of different elements and operates by fragments, flashes, scatterings. It is not a complete but rather a dislocated and detailed image/ imagining.

Statement prepared in collaboration with Claire Oboussier

Images from **Fragments** 1989
Courtesy Vongphrachanh Phaophanit

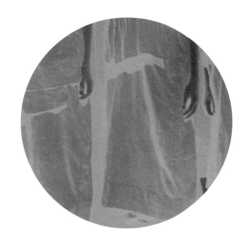

Fiona Rae

I more or less invent the paintings directly onto the canvas. Improvisation is an important element but my attitude is not that of an abstract painter. I don't think my paintings are 'universal' or 'pure' or anything like that — they're kind of phoney abstract — but I do always work on them upside-down, back-to-front and all that and I do end up with something I couldn't have envisaged or invented beforehand.

It would be nice to produce something that is a bit peculiar and not just about formal qualities. Endless invention of formal ideas gets a bit wearying after a while. Painting in general has an element of showing-off — I'd like people to think 'how did she do that bit?' — but it's boring when virtuosity is an end in itself.

I want an ambiguous standpoint; I like my paintings to look a bit uncomfortable. Some of them refuse to cooperate when you try to make out some kind of order or set-up. I suppose others have been too easily readable as one kind of thing and they didn't have that unsettling quality of something about to fall apart.

I don't have a strong belief in anything. I do think it's important to give some attention to dismantling one's prejudices. It's even useful to do the worst thing you can think of. Unfortunately there doesn't seem to have been much 'radical' art in recent years — it's been a bit of a let-down and as obvious as the most mawkish figurative painting.

I suppose I try to feel I can do what I want. To begin with I thought the idea of doing nine proper little abstract paintings on one canvas was quite funny, but it's not my prime motivating force to make a critique of other painting.

From a conversation with Fiona Rae, September, 1989

Untitled: Nine on Green 1989
Oil on canvas 213 x 182cm Courtesy the artist

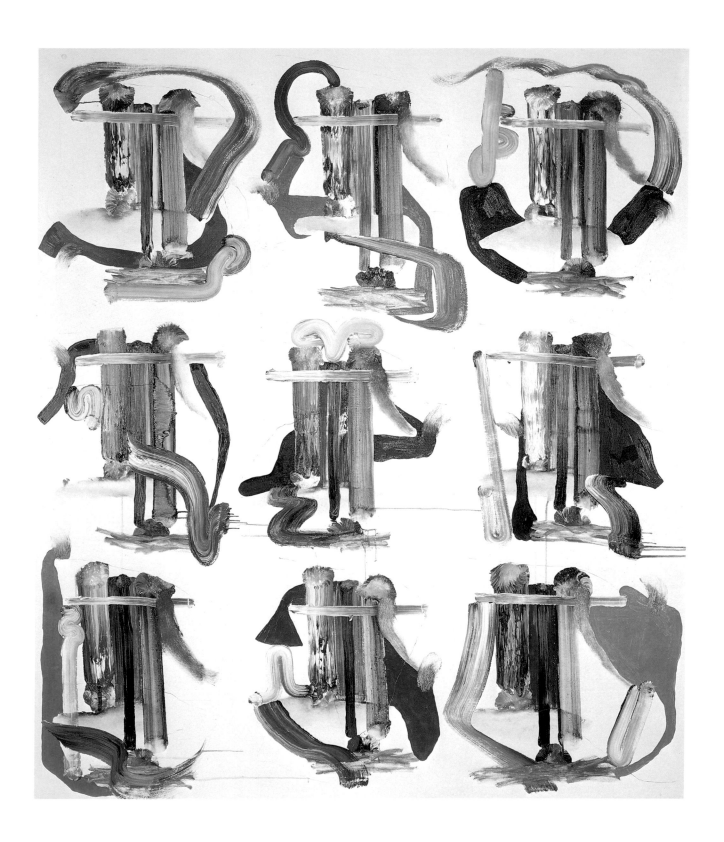

David Robilliard ✳

THE PEOPLE OF THE 90'S WILL BE JUST THE SAME
It's funny isn't it
all you've got is the natural urge
to lay down with someone
and say hello
in a very personal way
and yet life seems to offer
many other alternatives

TEND YOUR VINE
Don't be pathetic
you'll always regret it
but everything can't be
wonderful all the time
a head full of thoughts
the magic of the moment
and a later date
here comes the crunch
your bunch of grapes
have shrivelled and soured
it's within your power
to tend your vine

Life isn't good it's excellent 1987
Acrylic on canvas 122 x 122cm Courtesy Esther Friedman/Friedman-Guinness Gallery, Frankfurt

LIFE ISN'T GOOD

IT'S

EXCELLENT

David
Robilliard

ROBILART 1987

Caroline Russell

Strategies should establish in broad terms the courses of action that will be followed in order to achieve the marketing objectives. (Americans call this part of the process 'the game plan'.) The nature and character of the objectives should be reflected in the type of strategies chosen. For example, if the marketing objective is to establish a top-quality image over a given period of time, then the strategies will constantly feature 'quality' and all the surrounding attributes of quality, such as reliability, sophistication, attention to detail, customer service, and so on.

Marketing, Cameron, Rushton & Carson (Penguin 1988)

Display 22 1989
Spot U.V. varnish 12 microns x 16 x 12cm

Veronica Ryan

My works take on a patination from the history of their making. They are often remade over a period of time and are rather diary-like. The process of making work involves an evolution determined by a need to clarify and to be specific.

Sometimes the material takes on a tissue-like quality from my involvement with refining and reconstructing parts or fragments. The surface often has a crumpled quality, as in *Residue*. Sometimes this is because the piece started one life and ended with another. This is partly to do with the fact of the work carrying its own history and signature, a receptacle and trigger for memory.

I suppose memory for me is a way of trying to understand how I function now. Sometimes it's a specific event or thing recalled — and sometimes, memory is fantasy. My work doesn't necessarily describe literal objects or incidents but it does get mixed up with the way memory operates for me and with my conception of the poignant nature of human experience and history, with the area of one's internal being. We have to find a way of — not surfacing, so much, as not being completely consumed and overwhelmed. The past is coloured by what is happening now so memory is only a connection. I think the pieces are overlaid with a crust of time.

From a conversation with Veronica Ryan, October 1989

Residue 1988
Bronze 129 x 96 x 71cm Courtesy the artist

Lesley Sanderson

My paintings and drawings aim to be direct and easily read. Most of the work uses the self-portrait as a vehicle to confront the stereotype, to voice an opinion on racism, generally, personally and from the viewpoint of a woman. It's important that I use the self-image but as a social image rather than as an introverted self-portrait.

I consciously work in a very straightforward realistic way so that the image and its content aren't obscured. I want to challenge traditions of representation and feel this is most effectively done by working in a traditional, academic way. I take gestures, symbols, a look, a stance and use them in an unexpected or ambiguous way, thereby challenging by contradiction and irony.

The gaze of the person is always central to the work. It's meant to be challenging, rather than traditionally passive, it leaves no room for voyeurism and makes one aware of the figure in an unnerving, uncomfortable way. The person drawn or painted has control of the gaze, so that the act of looking is a two way activity.

I am concerned with challenging the idea of the 'exotic' and with trying to dispel the notion that the ethnic minorities and especially the Chinese in Britain are a 'homogeneous exotic category'. I think it's particularly important that non-white women are represented in a way that provides an alternative to National Geographic-type media representation of 'ethnic' women being exotic, submissive and readily available for the gaze. My work aims to provide a more contemporary image.

A Point of Contact 1987
Pencil on paper 208cm x 152 Courtesy the artist

Louise Scullion

The Amateur Scientist began when I heard about a spy who in the First World War would reconnoitre enemy territory by disguising himself as a bespectacled butterfly collector. He would set about encompassing the layout of enemy fortifications in the wings of his meticulously drawn butterflies, different spots and pairs of dots would denote where field-guns and machine-guns were positioned. Later I discovered that the spy in question was none other than Baden-Powell, better known for his exploits as founder of the British Scout Organisation. As it turned out the role of the lepidopterist was only one of his disguises, others he used took the form of a Naturalist, an Artist and once even a Ship-builder.

When posing as a Naturalist, he used the veins of a leaf to outline the positioning of field guns hidden amongst hilly territory. Where veins pointed to shady areas this indicated danger spots where oncoming troops might be ambushed. Shaded areas on their own indicated safe hide-outs. The central vein pointed in the direction of North from which to take compass-bearings. The aesthetics and the seeming insignificance of these drawings are, for me, truly fascinating.

Maps!

In earlier work I had done some reconnoitering myself, looking instead at the accidental gardening accomplished by the military landscapers of the Firth of Clyde area and at the curious lengths they would go to disguise their endeavours.

With these surveillance techniques at hand I began to look at the amino acids which for some years now have presented a similar fascination for me. I remember at school being told that they were the alphabet of proteins, the building blocks of life, and yet on the page their names and structural formulas seemed so simple. My knowledge and understanding of science is so limited that the mysteries of the microscopic world leave me awestruck. *The Amateur Scientist* is a little like a lay-person spy, adopting Baden-Powell's method of recording to spy instead, on science, in particular on the amino acids.

Louise Scullion, September 1989

The Amateur Scientist was initially commissioned for the Edinburgh Science Festival, April 1989

Tryptophan Bee from **The Amateur Scientist** 1988
Acrylic on paper with wax 22 x 15cm Courtesy the artist

Yolande Snaith

I feel an outsider in this society. My work has a cathartic function. It is a vital means for me to exist, to realise my human potential and communicate with others. I believe that the power of performance serves as a replacement for primitive ritualistic forms that contemporary society has discarded. My work is my way of creating this replacement for myself, those who work with me, and for those who witness it, however absurd it may be.

Themes and fascinations that constantly recur in this work are concerned with masculine and feminine attributes, repression of women, domesticity, obsessive behaviour, ritual, ceremony, military and religious figures, morality, archetypal images, power struggle and personal crisis. These often become synthesised within one image, for example, the opening figures in 'GERMS' combine Victorian sportswomen with Breugelian figures and puritan nuns whose faces are masked with chamber pots while they moo, chant and wail into them as animals, as tibetan monks, as distressed babies.

The subject matter begins to work for me when I feel an engaging tension between two or more elements, when there is both affinity and contradiction, the sweet and the sour, the beauty and the beast. This is when meaning ensues. I search for the absurdities, the ridiculous, an irresistible uncomfortableness. If it feels too nice then I know it is wrong. An image has the possibility of being simultaneously very funny and very disturbing, erotic and grotesque, dark and inviting. This work has many starting points. Various initial research processes travel alongside each other until I have to make compositional decisions. Then the synthesis begins, the fusion of one process with another, the layering of images, the choreography weaving the journey from one set of concerns to another, the image informing the movement, the movement animating the image.

My objective eye, my compositional thought process, is like a multi-layered painting with many sub-paintings. The overall shape of a piece is defined by the organisation of the layers. For example, 'GERMS' is structurally a process of dismantling one image to reveal another inside, like the deconstruction of a Russian doll. Each unravelled figure sets up a new episode with its own complex structure of meanings and associations, the component parts being: costumes and objects which carry particular associative and allegorical significances; the movement which animates these and controls their spatial, sculptural and configurative organisation; sound generated either by the voice, the impact and rhythm of the movement or some other musical source; the lighting which defines the architecture of the space, focuses the attention and suggests the ambience; film which explodes the senses of scale, detail, texture, time, place, movement and space. My aim is to create fusion, interdependency and play between these elements.

Yolande Snaith, October 1989

Germs: Advanced lessons in social skills
Performance, 1989

Gary Stevens

My training was originally in fine art and my performance work is a hybrid of theatre and sculpture. The current practice developed from installation work in the mid-seventies in which a text appeared as a report or document which fictionalised found objects. There followed a period of work in film where the text was spoken but still functioned as a commentary. Here the object which was affected by the text was the image itself that included, as an element, the speaker. The recent performance work extends this use of the text and exploits the problems that it creates for the representation of a speaking subject on the stage.

For the past four projects I have worked with different artists who bring with them their own distinctive practices. Some of them are experienced performers, others are not. Some have art backgrounds, others have theatre backgrounds.

Animal is an artificial psychological portrait. It plays with the problem of other minds. The speakers are seen as curious thinking objects. Familiar models are used to create an alien psychology; the ordinary behaviour of a dog or a child becomes strange or psychotic. The picture is further complicated by an attempt to make the work itself appear to be the product of an alien mind trying very hard to be human. The animal referred to in the title is the work itself.

The performance is a complex object which slowly takes shape and then has a logic and a life of its own. The performers are not playing individual characters so much as elements within this larger structure. In this case the work crucially doesn't come alive. It resembles the mechanical animals that appear in it. To make an issue of anthropomorphic projection, the animated objects have to fall between the mechanical and the motivated; between movement and action. Another aspect of the work introduces the idea of artificial intelligence or artificial life. The piece draws an equation between animate/inanimate, and living/dead. The audience (hopefully human?) fills in the gap.

The speakers are not characters, they don't own or know themselves. They are alien even to themselves. This effort to fragment the individual is done not just through the text but through the way that the action is played. There is an element of knowingness about the way things are done which detaches the performer from what he or she represents. It is akin to comic performance in this respect.

I like the work to seem primitive, casual and easy although it is built on a rigorous structure. I try to make all the elements of the piece reflexive, everything points back to itself. It is a way of addressing the question of materials in the theatre.

There are a number of themes running through the work. I am interested in the idea of a thinking thing becoming aware that it is the object of another's gaze and developing a self-image. There is a contrast between an agent who is oblivious of his actions and one who indulges in shameless vanity. Another theme is an inability to draw a distinction between someone who is absent and someone who is dead. A dog-like character pleads for someone to stay and is mortified by the sound of a door-bell chime that marks their departure. The work itself is an artificial organism which tries desperately to communicate beyond itself and fails. An ambiguous interior is established on the stage and the action is motivated by attempts to reach outside this space. Door bells and door mats draw a fake boundary, a letter is written that turns out to be indecipherable to the writer, an imaginary conversation takes place through a dead telephone. The work is like a machine that develops routines to portray its autism. Another characteristic of the piece is the performers' general failure to recognise each other or to see a face as expressive. Sympathy, empathy and alienation are all thrown up in the air. The closest the performers ever get to each other is through singing the lines of a song that they all slowly pick up as one of them tries to put a tune to Darwin's description of a laughing face.

Animal

Performance, ICA, November 1989

Linda Taylor

Slow Growth 1989
Hand made cotton paper, watercolour and pencil 195 x 167cm Courtesy the artist 8'high?

109

Peter Turley

Animals have no souls. Deep tracks are old ways. The land is a familiar mystery. There are patterns in the earth. The land contains the past. We contain our own past.

These pictures are more about people than animals. They are concerned with sameness. They are images of primitivism. They are pictures for a world which is not as civilised as it would like to believe. A world still learning, in which some animals are human and some humans are animals. A world with old ways and recurring patterns.

The artist has long since lost the monopoly of the image and should have reservations about inventing new ones in a world which constantly produces images of illusion about itself. Images which are immediate, transient, disposable, electronic, anonymous, invisible, impossible. Images which have the authority to make an event happen or not happen. The absence of a picture ensures that the event is less tangible, less significant, more marginal.

Seeing is believing. In a world in which the majority do not understand the nature of imagery but are familiar with images, a picture is a powerful instrument. Yesterday's news is dead meat.

Pictures of animals on the side of packages attempt to identify the contents as benign. A complicated world is reduced to a manageable form. Direct colours, linear images, abbreviations, a motif. Pictures of meat and animals on a sheet of paper used by a butcher to wrap real meat, real animals.

The idea of an animal is easy meat. Patient victims. Potently acquiescent. An ideal subject. Perfect for humane death by human manipulation. The murmur of commerce. Intimations of an organised society. A battered picture. A bleached, beaten animal. Slurry and bones and proteins. A discarded scrap. A category of rubbish. Dead in the carnivorous fluorescent supermarket light. An object which has fulfilled its function. Thrown away. Carefully ignored.

Recovered. Enlarged. Restored to life. Cast in black. A blood flood of crimson. A controlled sentimentality. More alive than ever, responding with unexpected emotion. Or merely slaughtered again in paint. Still passive. Dislocated heads and isolated bodies. Or simply a discovered style. Or excavations intended to uncover and release a buried iconography. The presence of a concealed emblem or symbol. The archaeology of imagery.

Peter Turley, October 1989

looks abstract at 1st.

The Butcher's Wrapping Paper 2 / Deep Tracks are Old Ways 1989
Acrylic on canvas 91 x 274cm Courtesy the artist

on white

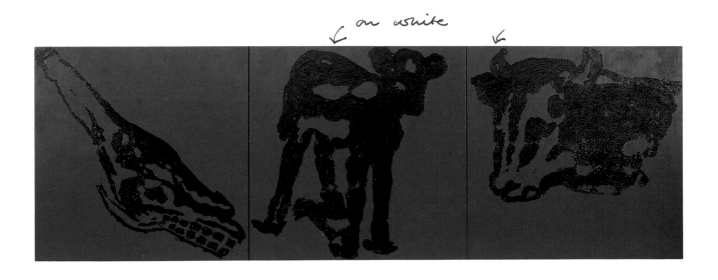

Shafique Uddin

I paint because there is a scene from my childhood in Bangladesh I want to recall, or something I've done in London or somewhere else I've been.

Memory is very important. The past is alive for me. My work is about my life — everything is personal, including the stories that I make for the works.

There are so many different ways of drawing. I choose to make my own type of works. I build up the surface in layers, using oil pastels, acrylics — anything.

The River in Winter is a memory of the flower fields of Bangladesh. In summer the landscape is dried out, now the river is full and flowing and the flowers are beginning to come alive.

From a conversation with Shafique Uddin, October 1989

The River in Winter 1989
Mixed media on board 61 x 61cm Courtesy the artist

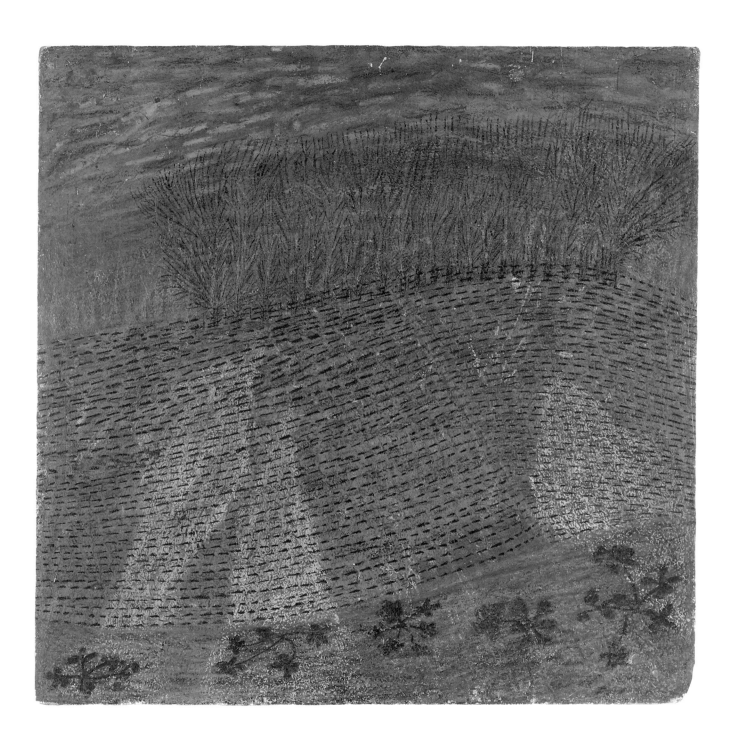

Rachel Whiteread

My work is concerned with making objects that are constructed from negative spaces: I use a direct casting technique to reveal the negative, manipulating apparently mundane domestic items to produce pieces that surpass their original identity. I think there is a correlation between these domestic items and our physicality.

- front of a fireplace
- a table

Rachel Whiteread, 1989

This work originally stemmed from a particular childhood memory: sitting inside wardrobes, the space and blackness, and of being in a completely dark room, the sense of a furry black space. As the pieces have developed I have tried to lose that sense of nostalgia. In the more recent pieces I am constructing the negative spaces. It was a positive and liberating decision when I realised that I could invent rather than having to be completely honest to the original. I use the furniture as a foundation for the pieces to develop.

I am making objects that are, I think, very much like tombs, the way things are incarcerated, how you know there is something inside but you never actually see what it is. It wasn't until I made *Yellow Leaf* that the sarcophagus reference became apparent.

The materials I use have always been important. Plaster is a dead material, but the surface is very sensitive, it picks up details, the stains and cobwebs that lay underneath the tables. It takes them and embalms them, leaving mummified space and a sense of silence.

From a conversation with Rachel Whiteread, September 1989

Yellow Leaf 1989
Plaster, wood, formica and polystyrene 150 x 74 x 94cm Courtesy Karsten Schubert Ltd.

Caroline Wilkinson

Interior does not represent an event; it is more a contemplation of a place, a domestic interior, which bears the traces and residue of human events. The structure is cyclical (with hiccups): there are two sequences like panning shots around a room, one in black and white, the other in colour, which stereotypically establish the passage of time. These are interspersed with shorter sections and details which refer more specifically to possible events and recollections, and the construction of a narrative.

The piece refers to both documentary photography and film and is situated somewhere between the two, both materially and structurally. Although the images are still, they are not photographs but transparencies projected on a scale which identifies them with film, and although my manipulation of sequence and duration approximates film, it is clear that these are resolutely immobile single images. I hoped that by leaning in two directions (or in on itself) the piece would have a certain formal self-consciousness, would refuse the seamless seduction of film whilst indicating a longing for that kind of completion. It is pervaded by a sense of loss.

In documentary photography, the photograph's main importance is its verisimilitude, its appearance of providing the evidence that something really did take place. But this characteristic is also the essential paradox of all photography: that at the moment of looking at it, the image seems to immortalise, to fix something gone forever — whether this is literally a person or thing no longer existing, or that very moment when light registered on the film in the camera. Awareness of this entails a poignant double bind of confusion and reassurance: what was witnessed in the present is now presented as ineluctably past.

Our relation with memory through images is complex and has much less to do with 'truth' than with contingency, substitution, fabrication. In *Interior* the pan around the room describes it, but how much can be remembered immediately afterwards, particularly when this is then qualified by what follows? We remember what we need to (except, what we cannot bear to remember we think we forget), but where is the need to remember this particular room? I wanted to show the limitations of descriptive analysis. Clarity and close scrutiny do not reveal 'more' unless a context for the significance of this kind of investigation is known and shared. Without this they are voyeuristic.

In the imagery there is an oscillation between a sense of the actuality and presentness of the visible world and a sense of reverie or dream. They overlap, disturb each other's presumed autonomy, propose that 'reality' is locatable, constructed in the interface between the two. In any system of representation something has always been left out, necessarily. There is no complete account, but it may say more than we think, may give access to a continuing submerged but tenacious formulation of emotional events.

Caroline Wilkinson, November 1989

Interior 1988
Tape-slide 9 minutes Courtesy the artist

Briefing For A Descent

One night, for example, the tanks of a huge neighbouring country came and occupied their country. The shock was so great, so terrible, that for a long time no one could think about anything else. It was August, and the pears in their garden were nearly ripe. The week before, Mother had invited the local pharmacist to come and pick them. He never came, never even apologised. The fact that Mother refused to forgive him drove Karel and Marketa crazy. Everybody's thinking about tanks, and all you can think about is pears, they yelled . . .

But are tanks really more important than pears? As time passed, Karel realised that the answer was not so obvious as he had once thought, and he began sympathising secretly with Mother's perspective — a big pear in the foreground and somewhere off in the distance a tank, tiny as a ladybug, ready at any moment to take wing and disappear from sight. So Mother was right after all: tanks are mortal, pears eternal.[1]

How do we evaluate the relative significance of different experiences? The global and the local (the background and the foreground) at times appear clearly separate and on other occasions almost interchangeable. The extraordinary scenes on television of the destruction of the Berlin Wall seemed to be more 'real' in a way than my experience of a working day in Glasgow. This question of our position, of where we literally and imaginatively stand is addressed by many of the works in the exhibition. Images and objects are drawn from personal experience or from what is close at hand. Differences in scale and important detail encourage a changing viewpoint. A recognition of the actual becomes evidence within a kind of artistic deconstruction, a metaphysical analysis of the processes by which things and ideas may have significance.

Jeffrey Dennis's painting *Briefing for a Descent* is not easy to describe. Imagine looking down at a number of squared-off blocks set closely together so that the thin gaps could be the streets of a city. The flat top of the central block has been partially stripped away to expose what looks like the back of a radio — a green board covered in a maze of wires and transistors. As if rubbed into the picture are small figures and scenes: a land-army girl carrying a pitchfork, an airman, someone planting something, a red London bus, and right on the surface, held down with putty-like daubs of paint, an image of wallpaper from a design by William Morris.

In Dennis's paintings daydreams and memory interrupt the visible world. Nothing seems definite but everything remains possible. In another work *Heartwood* (one of a series made up of smaller canvases joined together) the painting is filled with an image of processed peas, taken from a photograph on a can label. A few figures carrying out tasks or standing about occupy the top edges of a grey infrastructure that connects the different parts of the painting. The figures remain isolated from one another, absorbed only in what they are doing. Like holding opposed magnets together, Dennis creates landscapes of people and places that are permanently on the point of dissolution.

Helensburgh is a small town of mostly Victorian villas that overlooks the firth of Clyde twenty-five miles from Glasgow. Its neighbour is the Faslane Nuclear Submarine Base. The surrounding hillsides and roads have been transformed by what Louise Scullion describes as 'Military Landscaping'. Living in Helensburgh, Scullion has obliquely investigated the landscape's forced participation in camouflage and surveillance. As part of an installation at Third Eye Centre she covered the walls with wild plants and flowers that she had picked around Helensburgh. Each one was fixed to the wall at intervals with a strip of tape on which she had typed the date it was picked and where it was found: 20/7/88 Glenfruin; 23/7/88 Fort Matilda; 26/6/88 Camis Eskan Wood; 7/7/88 Garelochead; a mapping of disputed territory.

LOUISE SCULLION

The Amateur Scientist is based on her discovery that Baden-Powell, when he was in the army, used to spy on the enemy disguised as a butterfly collector. In minute detail he would draw out the enemy positions onto the wings of butterflies. Scullion ingeniously makes a connection between Baden-Powell's idiosyncratic surveillance techniques and her own fascination with the microscopic logic of molecular patterns. In the installation, curious pieces of furniture and pictures fill the Amateur Scientist's study. In one picture a fleet of Scottish fishing boats becomes an illustration of the structure of an Amino Acid.

John Mitchell places the empty Sony Television box against the wall of his studio. Behind the box is a section from a large billboard poster. Most of it is blank except for *The Evening Standard*'s red Eros logo and an excerpt from a listing of restaurants: Indian, Mexican Sri Lankan . . . On the box is a black shape representing a television screen.

Placed together, redundant objects and images provide evidence of the operations of society. The casualness of Mitchell's sculptures make the accidental and the deliberate indistinguishable. Every detail down to a box's packing instructions becomes potentially significant. In *Shipping the Rain Forest* two empty rectangular crates are placed vertically against a wall a couple of feet apart. Behind them are three sections of the same part of a billboard poster showing a choppy sea and the sky. Stamped on top of the crates is 'Made in Brazil'.

I don't see the works as sculptural. they are organisations of things — laid out in the simplest way possible.[2]

Kevin Henderson's *Propaganda Cradle* is like an autopsy. Wooden joists dismantled from a house during demolition have been placed in rows. They held the floorboards or supported the walls. You can see the pencil scribbles made by workmen marking them up for position. Now they lie flat out like coffins after a disaster, awaiting a decision about their future.

On each joist are three or four grey patches of paint. On to these has been painted an orange or blue diamond-shaped pattern of marks. The pattern is repeated eighty-nine times. The implication of meaning is present even if we are unable to decode it. (The marks derive from a perpetual calendar originating in a 12th-century Ottoman manuscript.) At one end an industrial pallet makes a low platform. Each of its boards is painted alternate blue and orange in bright oil paint.

The imitation white fur glimmers opaquely. Like something Alice might have contemplated on her adventures through the looking glass, six enormous spoons stand side by side in a shallow box. Ten feet high by eight feet across, the plywood construction is hidden beneath a layer of exuberant white fur. Eric Bainbridge's *More Blancmange* is an unlikely metaphor for the expectation of meaning. Seductively it promises: more blancmange, more sculpture more meaning! But what kind of meaning? Bainbridge brilliantly implicates both object and meaning within a potentially weary cycle of production and consumption.

Another work on the same scale looks like a Constructivist sculpture, but is actually modelled from a section of polystyrene Hi-Fi packaging, its formal aesthetics conditioned not by the artist but by our expectations. Lying on Bainbridge's work table is a small object about one inch across. Its only remarkable feature is a five-pointed star in slight relief, as if it was a miniaturized Soviet mausoleum. This tiny object — a cheap container for a ring — is to be the source for the next sculpture.

Taking everyday domestic furniture, Rachel Whiteread makes a direct plaster cast of the spaces inside the objects she selects. Sometimes part of the object is incorporated (through being left in its original position) in the final work. One of her most intriguing works has emerged from a 1960s yellow formica table with flaps. The central section is retained, supported not by the legs but by the solid off-white plaster, cast into the space underneath the table.

When the site at Pompeii was excavated, spaces were discovered in the solidified lava made by the bodies of victims before they disintegrated in the heat. From these, casts were made of the bodies which had once occupied them.

Whiteread's works have a peculiar sense of absence. But they also confront us as new objects reflecting the outward edges and planes of the furniture from which they were born. The effect of this mute occupancy is unexpectedly physical. Spaces we are used to moving through no longer exist. The solid plaster seems to absorb the surrounding air.

Joanna Kirk's curious pastel drawings question how images are able to communicate meaning. Sections and excerpts from photographs found in magazines are squared-up and enlarged. The images she chooses, for instance interiors and gardens from *Country Life* are already banal and anaesthetised. Re-presented they seem to be almost empty of meaning, the exacting detail revealing only the fact of transcription. The content becomes our doubts about their communicative value.

In recent works Kirk only partially re-presents the original image. In a drawing taken from a magazine photograph of four Catholic cardinals, Kirk omits their heads and hands and includes only their laps and sleeves draped in ceremonial gowns. Attention is focussed on their postures, their gesticulating sleeves and the elaborately detailed lacework which covers their garments. In cutting short the expected process of representation. Kirk sustains our interest through the virtuosity of her handling of pastel. The success of the illusion resuscitates our ability to believe that the cardinals have some form of existence outside the picture, except that, without their heads and hands, the outward signs of spiritual authority are literally reduced to the material.

Like Kirk's, Peter Turley's work investigates how meaning operates in relation to representational images which have become distanced from their original source. In his first series of works he painted images taken from wine labels of villages and chateaux onto flattened cardboard boxes. Much enlarged, these normally disregarded images struggle to 'mean' something.

In his new work on canvas, Turley has reproduced images of animals taken from wrappers and boxes used by the meat trade. In one painting the head of a cow is massively enlarged onto a six foot square canvas. Close up it appears as an abstract arrangement of black and white paint marks. Only at a distance does the image come into definition: the head of a cow apparently in pain. The image is no longer an empty sign. In recovering meaning, Turley exposes a pathos brought about by our realisation of the loss which has occurred between the original source (a drawing or photograph of a live animal) and the irony of its final impoverished representation.

A camera takes us through the city late at night. A woman's voice explains. Her mother, who returned to the West Indies ten years ago, has written to her. She is thinking of returning now to London. How should she reply to the letter? What kind of city would her mother be coming back to?

My thoughts were the London you left behind is disappearing, perhaps forever, and I don't know if you will want to return to the new one. You wanted to leave before things fell apart between us, now the city is falling apart you want to come back, it may be too late.[3]

Paul Gilroy: *This is a city which, like many of the other once great cities of the over-developed world, has been de-centered in its most radical way, fragmented so that it isn't just a matter of different discreet communities inhabiting different parts of that city and filling out the parts of that city with their own cultures but inhabiting those spaces in a way which is mutually antagonistic, which is fortified, and together with that fortification you also find an extraordinary change in which people are able to inhabit the same space, to be physically proximate and yet to live in different worlds.*[4]

The Black Audio Film Collective's *Twilight City* is a collage of images and opinions. London (the city) is both an imaginative space, in which thoughts and feelings take up residence, and a fragmented physical reality.

WILLIE DOHERTY

Another City. On the exposed end of wall of a row of houses in large black letters: YOU ARE NOW ENTERING FREE DERRY. Beyond lies the bogside, a shallow valley of back to back low-rise housing, the heart of the Nationalist / Republican community. In one of Willie Doherty's photoworks we are looking across this valley of rooftops and smoking chimneys. Printed in black capitals on the photograph is the work STIFLING, below it in smaller white lettering SURVEILLANCE. The carefully spaced letters stay on the surface of the photograph and, at the same time, hover above the rooftops. Below these two words, across the front of the first housing block: LAST HOURS OF DAYLIGHT.

Doherty's work employs language as an expression of attitudes and feelings about places. Sue Clifford (of the arts/environmental group *Common Ground*) has made an interesting distinction between the use of the words 'site' and 'place'. 'Site', she argues, is a word used by architects and developers. It tends to ignore people and history. 'Place', on the other hand, is about people's lives and their relationship with a part of the landscape. Willie Doherty's earlier works use the language of place — his choice of words evoking experiences and common emotions. In contrast, a series of works made in Belfast adopts the language of site, the language of control. The work in the exhibition from this new series is the two-panelled *Sever* and *Isolate*. *Sever* consists of the word over a photograph of the dual carriageway which was deliberately sunk between East and West Belfast. *Isolate* shows the meshed-in bridge which provides a crossing over the divide.

Since 1987, Locky Morris has worked on projects at Pilot's Row Community Centre in the Bogside. In a small hallway near the entrance five seven-foot cones made of painted cardboard — the beams of searchlights — taper upwards, at their top end are small toy-like wooden helicopters. When I first visited the city I looked over the river from the station to the centre. An army helicopter hovered above the city, like a dragonfly. At night, I was told, their searchlights are able to trace down streets one by one.

Another sculpture is made of metal dustbin lids, placed side by side, their handles fixed outwards from the wall. The lids have been burnt and are streaked with dull shades of red, orange and brown. Running across the lids is a rough-edged deep band of black tar, as if an armoured personnel carrier had run over them. But as you come closer the tar becomes the outline of a barricade of figures, stretching in each direction until the dustbin lids run out.

In Northern Ireland, ideas and emotions are like nerve endings exposed on the surface of the landscape. Doherty and Morris's works exist within this landscape but at one remove from the disorienting reports of the media. Their art gives time and space to the viewer to participate in a process of re-evaluation.

I wait to discover what the next thing is for me to do. It's not separate from my life but parallels discoveries I am making all the time about my own sense of truth in life. [5]

Linda Taylor holds up one of the small glass casements which will make up the new work. Inside the soldered rectangular frame is a cellular structure cut from red paper. Fixed together, the casements will form the shape of a cross measured to correspond to the artist's height and the span of her outstretched arms. A working drawing shows the cells delineate in an image of a tree, its many branches sprouting awkwardly from the top of a thick trunk.

The shape of the cross represents the place of suffering within change. Like a controlled nervous system, the image embodies the artist's psychological and spiritual growth: the fragile becoming strong.

Tooting Bec Hospital in South London is a series of large rambling Victorian buildings. The patients are gradually being moved out into the community or to other hospitals. Whole blocks are decaying and empty. At the end of a disused ward Melanie Counsell has built an installation. Most of the space is not visible, enclosed by a curtain, like those used to separate patients from each other. Beneath the curtain is a shallow footbath constructed of white tiles. This is a few inches deep in water. The curtain rail has been connected to a water supply and then punctured at intervals. Water is dripping onto the tops of the curtains. The gradual passage of water downwards can be traced in the stains which sweep outwards over the curtain.

Counsell first used water at her degree show at the Slade. In part of the basement she radically altered the experience of the place by diverting the drainage system. Drain covers were replaced by glass. Water slid and streamed over the reinforced glass roof. A metal tank, full to the brim with water, contained a submerged industrial fan. Out of the ventilation slits of four green metal lockers water seeped onto the stone floor.

For the exhibition, Counsell is modifying a work constructed for Matt's Gallery in the East End of London. At Matt's the floor has been scraped of grey paint. The long window has been boarded up. Beneath it, occupying the base of the wall is a white tiled 'valley'. Slumped in this is a large rolled-up carpet. Above the carpet and tiles are thirteen 3″ x ¼″ copper pipes suggesting the source of the water that can be seen at the carpet's bottom edges. In front about three feet from the ground, a wire suspends a section of flowery chintz curtain that is rucked up as if it was washing caught up and disarranged in the wind.

Domestic associations are acknowledged with a surprising decorativeness: the blackish scarred floor, the damp lichen-green carpet, the pink and green of the chintz. It is as if Counsell wanted her materials to take pleasure in being themselves. White mould is gathering across the top of the carpet. The incidental and insignificant have their own implicit presence and meaning.

Vong Phaophanit is a political refugee from Laos. Since 1971, the only communication with his family has been through letters and snapshots. Images from these are projected onto the moving blades of electric fans. The images are fragments, details: 'a hand, an element of background, a piece of clothing.'[6]

Phaophanit's work is about looking closer, searching for meaning, making a place for the personal, social and political. The memories he shares are of incompleteness. The traffic of cool air runs counter to our gaze. Images flicker across the temporary screen.

The work is based on nothing, no strict discourse, no rules, except perhaps a new subjectivity . . . If there is an object, an aim, it is to start from a point and to lead outwards from there.[7]

ANDREW NAIRNE

1. Milan Kundera. *The Book of Laughter and Forgetting* 1978 (English translation 1980). Penguin Books, London 1983. p.29.

2. Kevin Henderson. From an edited interview with Euan McArther. *SCATTER*. Third Eye Centre, Glasgow, 1989.

3. Voice Over from Black Audio Film Collective. *Twilight City*. B.A.F.C./Channel 4. 1989.

4. Paul Gilroy. As above. The film is intercut with studio-shot interviews.

5. Linda Taylor. From a statement, *SCATTER*, Third Eye Centre, Glasgow, 1989.

6. Vong Phaophanit, Claire Oboussier, *Fragments*, September 1989.

7. Vong Phaophanit. From a statement, 1988.

Artists' biographies

Where artists are represented by dealers or agents, their names appear in bold after the general biographical information and before the list of residencies and exhibitions. An asterisk after an exhibition indicates that a catalogue or pamphlet was published. The numbers after the artists' names refer to pages in this publication.

The biographers information is followed by a brief list of the major periodicals which cover new art in Britain.

LEA ANDREWS 34

Born 1958, Sonning Common, Oxon.

1981-82 Banbury School of Art
1982-85 Brighton Polytechnic
1985-87 Slade School of Fine Art, London

Lives in London

RESIDENCIES
1988 Tooting Bec Hospital, London

ONE PERSON EXHIBITIONS
1989 *A Change in Thinking*, Battersea Arts Centre, London

SELECTED GROUP EXHIBITIONS
1985-86 *Imposters*, Interim Art, London and tour*
1986 *My Self, Our Selves*, Aspex Gallery, Portsmouth*
1988 *Lea Andrews and Robert Mabb*, Riverside Studios, London*
        Something Solid, Cornerhouse, Manchester*
1988-89 *Behold the Man*, Stills Gallery, Edinburgh and tour*

ERIC BAINBRIDGE 36

Born 1955, County Durham

1974-77 Newcastle Polytechnic
1978-81 Royal College of Art, London

Lives in London

Salvatore Ala Gallery, New York

ONE PERSON EXHIBITIONS
1978 Ayton Basement, Newcastle
1982 Spectro Gallery, Newcastle
1985 *Currents*, Institute of Contemporary Art, Boston*
        Air Gallery, London*
        Salvatore Ala Gallery, New York
1986 *Viewpoints: Eric Bainbridge*, Walker Art Centre,

Minneapolis*
        Galeria Salvatore Ala, Milan
1987 Karsten Schubert Gallery, London
        Holemasters, Salvatore Ala Gallery, New York*,
        The Centre for the Arts, Muhlenberg College,
        Allentown, Pennsylvania
1988 Salvatore Ala Gallery, New York
1989-90 Stedelijk Museum, Amsterdam*

SELECTED GROUP EXHIBITIONS
1981 *New Contemporaries*, ICA, London
1982 *Before It Hits The Floor*, ICA, London*
        British Drawings, Hayward Annual, Hayward Gallery, London*
1983 *Pagan Echoes*, Riverside Studios, London
1984 *Whitechapel Open*, London
        Various Madness, Ian Birksted Gallery, London
1985 *Anniottanta*, Galeria Comunale d'Arte Moderna, Bologna*
        Nuove Trame dell'Arte, Castello Colonna di Genazzano, Italy*
        Synonyme fur Skulptur, Neue Galerie am Landesmuseum
        Joanneum, Graz, Austria*
1986 *Meta-Fur*, Sharpe Gallery, New York
        Whitechapel Open, London
1987 *Arte e Alchemia*, Venice Biennale*
        Animal Art, Steirischer Herbst '87, palais Attens, Graz, Austria*
        Revelations for the Hands, Leeds City Art Galleries touring exhibition*
1988 *Walk Out to Winter*, Bess Cutler Gallery, New York*
        Installment: Five British Artists, Rafinerie du Plank, Brussels
        l'ABCD de l'art moderne L'Institut Néerlandais, Paris*
1989 New Acquisitions, The Stedelijk Museum, Amsterdam

BLACK AUDIO FILM COLLECTIVE 38

Black Audio Film Collective is an ACTT franchised film and video workshop, currently making programmes for Channel Four Television.
Members of the Collective: John Akomfrah, Reece Auguiste, Edward George, Lina Gopaul, Avril Johnson, David Lawson, Trevor Mathison
Established 1983

AWARDS
        Handsworth Songs
1987 The First Paul Robeson Prize for Cinema, at the Fespaco Film Festival in Burkina Faso — March 1987
        The British Film Institute Grierson Award for Social Documentary
        The Kodak Newcomers Award, London
        Testament
1989 The Special Jury Prize at the African Film Festival

of Perugia, Italy
An Honourable Mention at the San Francisco
International Film Festival
A Special Mention for the use of archive film and
music at FESPACO, Burkina Faso
Twilight City

1989   The Grand Prize at the Melbourne International
Film Festival
The Josef Von Sternberg Prize for the most
original film of the festival, Mannheim
International Film Festival
The God Hugo for Documentary, Chicago
International Film Festival

PRODUCTIONS
1988-85   Expeditions, tape-slide
1986   Handsworth Songs, 16mm, 52min, premiered at
Birmingham and London International Film
Festivals
1988   Testament, 80 min, Cannes International Film
Festival, Festivals in Cairo, Carthege, Chicago,
London, Ouagadougou, San Francisco and Tokyo
1989   Twilight City

FILM FAMILIARISATION COURSES
1984   Visions and Revisions, a series of workshops on
Black film-making
1985   Looking Black, a practical, theoretical and
analytical course around cinema, race and
aesthetics
1987   Reimagining, a 16mm course examining the
principles of movement in film production

MEDIA CONSULTANCY
1985-89   Birmingham Film and Television Festival
Individual film-makers and groups

SEMINARS AND CONFERENCES
1984   Cultural Identities Conference
1989   British Film Institute Regional Conference

SCREENINGS
1986   The Positive Image, Nottingham City Lights
Rio Cinema London — Black and Third World
Focus

SONIA BOYCE   40

Born 1962, London

1980   East Ham College of Art and Technology
Stourbridge College of Art and Technology,
Birmingham

Lives in London

ONE PERSON EXHIBITIONS
1986   *Conversations*, Black Art Gallery, London
Sonia Boyce, Air Gallery, London and tour*
1988   *Recent Work*, Whitechapel Art Gallery, London

SELECTED GROUP EXHIBITIONS
1985   *Room at the Top*, Nicola Jacobs Gallery, London*
Blackskin/Bluecoat, Bluecoat Gallery, Liverpool
No More Little White Lies, Chapter Arts Centre,
Cardiff
Reflections, Riverside Studios, London
Thin Black Line, ICA, London*
From Generation to Generation, Black Art
Gallery, London
1986   *Some of Us Are Brave — All of Us Are Strong*,
Black Art Gallery, London
From Two Worlds, Whitechapel Art Gallery,
London*
Caribbean Expressions in Britain, Leicestershire
Museum & Art Gallery and tour
State of the Art, ICA, London and tour*
A Cabinet of Drawings, Gimpel Fils Gallery,
London
1987   *The Image Employed: the Use of Narrative in
Black Art*, Cornerhouse Gallery, Manchester*
Critical Realism, Nottingham Castle Museum & Art
Gallery and tour
1988   *The Essential Black Art*, Chisenhale Gallery,
London*
The Impossible Self, The Winnipeg Art Gallery,
Canada*
Along the Lines of Resistance, Cooper Gallery,
Barnsley & Rochdale Art Gallery*
The Thatcher Years, Angela Flowers Gallery,
London*
Fashioning Feminine Identities, University of Essex
Gallery, Colchester
1989   *The Other Story*, Hayward Gallery, London

JYLL R BRADLEY   42

Born 1966

1984-85   Canterbury College of Art, Kent
1985-88   Goldsmiths' College, London

Lives in London

SELECTED GROUP EXHIBITIONS
1986   The Showroom, London
1988   Goldsmiths' College Degree Show
Flaxman Gallery, London
Show and Tell, Riverside Studios, London*
1989   Marlene Eleini Gallery, London
Interim Art, London

**Work in the exhibition realised with the help of
John Marlow of Marlow Mobile**

KATE BRIGHT   44

Born 1964, Suffolk

1983-84   Ipswich School of Art
1985-88   Camberwell School of Arts and Crafts

Lives in London

ONE PERSON EXHIBITION
1989   Galerija Arts, Ljubljana*

SELECTED GROUP EXHIBITIONS
1987   London Institute Gallery
1988   Touring Show, Slovinia, Yugoslavia*
1989   Homerton College, Cambridge*

MELANIE COUNSELL 46

Born 1964, Cardiff

1982-83   South Glamorgan Institute of Higher Education
1983-86   South Glamorgan Institute, BA Hons. Fine Art
1986-88   Slade School of Fine Art

Lives in London

Matt's Gallery, London

AWARDS
1988   Boise Travel Scholarship
1989   Whitechapel Artists Awards

ONE PERSON EXHIBITION
1989   Matt's Gallery, London

SELECTED GROUP EXHIBITIONS
1988   Six Artists, Three Shows, Anthony Reynolds
        Gallery, London

MATTHEW DALZIEL 48

Born 1957, Irvine, Scotland

1981-85   Duncan of Jordanstone College of Art, Dundee
1985-87   Gwent College of Higher Education
1987-88   Glasgow School of Art

Lives in Glasgow

AWARDS AND RESIDENCIES
1985   The Dalgetty Dunn Travelling Scholarship
1988-89 Artist in Residence, Shell UK Exploration and
        Production

SELECTED GROUP EXHIBITIONS
1985   The Royal Scottish Academy, Edinburgh
        New Generation Show, Compass Gallery,
        Glasgow
1987   Forces, Gwent College of Art, University College,
        Cardiff
        Special Edition, Ffotogallery, Cardiff
1988   Mysterious Coincidences, New British Colour
        Photography, Photographers' Gallery, London
        and tour*
        Personal Visions, New Scottish Photography, Stills
        Gallery, Edinburgh
        New Works, Newberry Gallery, Glasgow School

of Art
        Death, Kettle's Yard & Cambridge Darkroom, and
        tour*
        Touching On Nature, Fife Mobile Gallery Touring
        Exhibition
1989   Ways of Telling, Mostyn Gallery, Llandudno
        North Wales and Old Library Gallery Cardiff*
        Watching, Collaborative work with Martin Pigott,
        Shell UK. Exploration and Production, St Fergus
        Gas Plant, Peterhead, Scotland.
        Unseen Unheard But Measured, Installation, Shell
        UK. Exploration and Production, St Fergus Gas
        Plant, Peterhead, Scotland.
        Through Photography, experimental photography
        show. Third Eye Centre, Glasgow and on Tour. *
        Artists In Industry, Aberdeen Art Gallery and The
        MacLaurin Gallery, Ayr. *

IAN DAVENPORT 50

Born 1966, Sidcup, Kent

Lives in London

Waddington Galleries, London

1984-85   Northwich College of Art and Design
1985-88   Goldsmiths' School of Art, London

SELECTED GROUP EXHIBITIONS
1985   Young Contemporaries, Whitworth Art Gallery,
        Manchester
1988   Freeze, London Docklands*
        Karsten Schubert Gallery, London
1989   Current, Swansea Arts Workshop, Swansea
        West Norwood 1, West Norwood Railway
        Archway Arches 7, 8 & 9, London

GRENVILLE DAVEY 52

Born 1961, Launceston, Cornwall

1981-85   Exeter College of Art and Design
           Goldsmiths' School of Art, London

Lives in London

Lisson Gallery, London

ONE PERSON EXHIBITIONS
1987   Lisson Gallery, London
1989   Lisson Gallery, London*
        Primo Piano, Rome

SELECTED GROUP EXHIBITIONS
1986   Showroom Gallery, London
1988   19&&, Centre National d'Art Contemporain de
        Grenoble
        Aperto, Venice Biennale
        Artists and Curators, John Gibson Gallery, New

York
British Artists, Tanya Grunert Gallery, Cologne
1989   *Ateliers en Liberte, 1989, Aspects de la Jeune*
Sculpture Europeenne, Fondation Cartier, Paris
Lia Rumma, Naples
Prospect '89, Kunstverein, Frankfurt
Melencolia, Galerie Grita Insam, Vienna
Deste Foundation, Athens*
A Perspective on Contemporary Art — Colour
and/or Monochrome, National Museum of Modern
Art, Tokyo*
Sala Uno, Rome*
1990   *Objectives: The New Sculpture*, Newport Harbor
Museum, California*

CATHY de MONCHAUX 54

Born 1960, London

1980-83   Camberwell School of Art
1985-87   Goldsmiths' College, London

Lives in London

Laure Genillard Gallery, London

AWARDS
1988   Steinberger Group Award
Whitechapel Open
1989   Greater London Arts Individual Artists Award

ONE PERSON EXHIBITIONS
1985   Winchester Gallery
1988   Mario Flecha Gallery, London
Artist of the Day, Angela Flowers Gallery, London
1990   Laure Genillard Gallery

SELECTED GROUP EXHIBITIONS
1986-88 *Whitechapel Open*, London
1987   Mario Flecha Gallery
1988   *Riverside Open*, London
The Invisible Man, Goldsmiths' Gallery, London*
1989   *Promises, Promises*, Serpentine Gallery, London*
It's a Still Life, South Bank Centre touring show*
Group Show, Galerie Conrads, Neuss, West
Germany
Two-person Show, Goldsmiths' Gallery, London*
Barcelona Biennial 1989, Spain*

JEFFREY DENNIS 58

Born 1958, Colchester

Lives in London

Salvatore Ala Gallery, New York

ONE PERSON EXHIBITIONS
1979   5 Dryden Street Gallery, London
University of Essex, Colchester

1983   Tom Allen Centre, London
1984   Galeria Salvatore Ala, Milan
1985   Salvatore Ala Gallery, New York
1985-6   Salvatore Ala Gallery, New York
1986   Galeria Salvatore Ala, Milan
Whitechapel Art Gallery, London*
1987   Salvatore Ala Gallery, New York
1988   Salvatore Ala Gallery, New York

SELECTED GROUP EXHIBITIONS
1978   Stowells Trophy Exhibition, Royal Academy,
London
1979   Premises Art Centre, Norwich
1980   Whitechapel Open, London
1981   Bedford Way Gallery, Institute of Education,
London
1982   *New Art Platform 2*, Midland Gallery,
Nottingham
Whitechapel Open, London
1984   *Dreams and False Alarms*, Riverside Studios,
London
1985   *Walking and Falling*, Plymouth Arts Centre,
Kettle's yard, Cambridge and Interim Art,
London*
Between Identity and Politics, Gimpel Fils,
London*
Darlington Arts Centre and Gimpel
Weitzenhoffer, New York
Summer Exhibition Salvatore Ala, New York
Summer In the City, Ikon Gallery, Birmingham
Anniottanta, Bologna, Italy*
Nuove Trame dell'Arte, Castello Colonna,
Genazzano, Italy*
1986   *Force of Circumstance*, P.P.O.W, New York
Correspondentie Europa, Stedelijk Museum,
Amsterdam*
Jeffrey Dennis, Alan Green, Alison Wilding,
Third Eye Centre, Glasgow
Prospect '86 Frankfurter Kunstvereins im
Steinernen Haus und der Schirn am
Romerberg, Frankfurt*
Small Format, Lang & O'Hara Gallery, New York
A Look at Painting, R.C Erpf Gallery, New York
Whitechapel Open, London
Sur Les Murs, Foundation Cartier, Jouy-en-Josas,
France*
1987   *Comic Iconoclasm*, ICA, London*
1988   *Object and Image: Aspects of British Art in the*
'80s, City Art Gallery, Stoke-on-Trent*
Inside/Outside, Castle Museum, Nottingham*
Figuring Out the Eighties, Laing Art Gallery,
Newcastle*

WILLIE DOHERTY 60

Born 1959, Derry

1977-81   Ulster Polytechnic, Belfast

Lives in Derry

ONE PERSON EXHIBITIONS
1980   Orchard Gallery, Derry
1982   Orchard Gallery, Derry
        SIREN, slide installation, A.R.E., Belfast
1986   Oliver Dowling Gallery, Dublin
        Stone Upon Stone, Redemption!, Derry
1987   The Town of Derry, photoworks, A.R.E., Belfast
1988   Two Photoworks, Third Eye Centre, Glasgow
        Colour Works, Oliver Dowling Gallery, Dublin
1990   Ffotogallery, Cardiff*
        Orchard Gallery, Derry
        Third Eye Centre, Glasgow
        New Work, Oliver Dowling Gallery, Dublin
        Matt's Gallery, London*

SELECTED GROUP EXHIBITIONS
1981   Performance, Work Made Live, N.C.A.D., Dublin
        Irish Exhibition of Living Art, Douglas Hyde
        Gallery, Dublin
1982   Performance, Live Work, Crescent Arts Centre,
        Belfast
        Photographic Works, King Street Gallery, Bristol
        New Artists New Works, Orchard Gallery,
        Derry*
1983   New Artists New Works, Projects Arts Centre,
        Dublin
        Performance, Artspace, Cork
        Guinness Peat Aviation Exhibition, Douglas Hyde
        Gallery, Dublin
        Days and Nights, slide work, Art and Research
        Exchange, Belfast
1985   Points of View, The Heritage Library, Derry
1986   G.P.A. Exhibition, The Royal Hospital,
        Kilmainham, Dublin*
1987   Oliver Dowling Gallery, Dublin
        Directions Out, Douglas Hyde gallery, Dublin*
        North West ArtistS Association, Heritage Library,
        Derry
        A Line of Country, Cornerhouse, Gallery,
        Manchester*
        The State of the Nation, Herbert Art Gallery,
        Coventry*
        Critics' Choice, City Art Gallery, Limerick
        N.W.A.A., Foyle Gallery, Dublin
        Oliver Dowling Gallery, Dublin
1988   Ireland/Germany Exchange, The Guinness Hop
        Store, Dublin*
        The Crawford Gallery, Cork and City Art
        Gallery, Limerick
        Three Artists, Battersea Arts Centre, London
        Matter of Facts, La Musee des Beaux Arts, Nantes
        and La Musee d'Art Moderne, Saint Etienne*
        Oliver Dowling Gallery, Dublin
1989   Ireland/Germany Exchange, The Ulster Museum,
        Belfast and Wurzburg, Bonn, Erlangen, Frankfurt
        Matter of Facts, Metz pour la Photographie, Metz
        Through the Looking Glass, The Barbican Art
        Gallery, London*
        Internationale Foto-Triennale, Esslingen, West
        Germany*

        Oliver Dowling gallery, Dublin
1990   Salama Caro Gallery, London

MONA HATOUM 62

Born 1952, Beirut, Lebanon

1987-79   Byam Shaw School of Art, London
1979-81   Slade School of Art, London

Lives in London

AWARDS AND RESIDENCIES
1982   Greater London Arts Award
1984   Artist in Residence, Western Front Art Centre,
        Vancouver, Canada
1985   Arts Council of Great Britain Video Bursary
1986   Artist in Residence, 9.1.1. Contemporary Art
        Centre, Seattle, USA
1986-87 Artist in Residence, Chisenhale Dance Space,
        London
1988   Artist in Residence, Western Front Art Centre,
        Vancouver, Canada
1989-92 Senior Research Fellow in Fine Art, South
        Glamorgan Institute of Higher Education, Cardiff

SELECTED EXHIBITIONS,
SCREENINGS AND PERFORMANCE
1981   New Contemporaries, ICA, London
        The Basement, Newcastle*
        Video Maart, Jan Van Eyck Studio, Maasrtricht,
        Holland*
        Women Live, London Film-makers' Co-op
        Reflections, Nine Women Artists, Aspex Gallery,
        Portsmouth*
        Canada Performance Tour
        Telefonmusik, Wiencouver IV, Live Video
        transmission between Vancouver and Vienna*
1984   Second International Festival of Performance,
        South Hill Park Arts Centre, Bracknell*
        The Franklin Furnace, New York
        Canada Performance Tour
1985   Festival of Video Art, SAW Gallery, Ottawa,
        Canada*
        Kunst mit Eigen-SInn, Museum Moderner Kunst,
        Vienna*
        Roadworks, Brixton Gallery, London*
        Orchard Gallery, Northern Ireland
1986   New Work, Newcastle '86, Laing Art Gallery*
        Next: Tomorrow, Kettle's Yard and Cambridge
        Darkroom, Cambridge*
        Live Video, Performance Festival, Time Based
        Arts, Amsterdam, Holland
        Identity/Desire, Representing the Body, Scottish
        Arts Council touring exhibition*
        Channel 6 Video Festival, ICA, London*
        Conceptual Clothing, Ikon gallery, Birmingham
        and tour*
1987   Forced Flight, Installation/performance,
        Chisenhale Dance Space, London

At the Edge installation, Air Gallery, London*
Figures, Cambridge Darkroom and tour*
Eleventh Hong Kong International Film Festival
State of the Nation, Herbert Art Gallery, Coventry*
Trans-Positions, Leeds City Art Gallery*
National Review of Live Art, Riverside Studios, London*
New Work, No Definition, Third Eye Centre, Glasgow*
Siting Technology, Walter Phillips Gallery, Banff, Alberta, Canada*
The Elusive Sign, The Arts Council/The British Council, Tate Gallery, and international tour*
Dislocations, Kettle's Yard, Cambridge*

1988 *Essential Black Art*, Chisenhale Gallery, London and tour.*
Nationalisms: Women and the State, A Space, Toronto, Canada
Siting Technology, Mackenzie Art Gallery, Regina, Canada*
Metro Billboard Project '88, Projects UK, Newcastle and tour.
Edge '88 International Festival of Experimental Art, London*
Installations, Cornerhouse gallery, Manchester
In an Unsafe Light, Ikon Gallery, Birmingham*
32nd London Film Festival
Along the Lines of Resistance, Cooper Gallery, Barnsley and tour

1989 *Electric Eyes*, Film and Video Umbrella touring exhibition*
Video Positive, Merseyside's International Video Festival, Bluecoat Gallery, Liverpool
Video Fest '89, Berlin Video Festival*
Filmfest D.C., Third Annual Washington D.C. International Film Festival*
5eme Festival International de Films et Videos de Femmes de Montreal
The Light at the End, The Showroom, London
Intimate Distance, Photographers' Gallery, London and tour*

KEVIN HENDERSON 64

Born 1963, Singapore

1981-86 Gray's School of Art, Aberdeen
1982-83 Oregon State University

Lives in Edinburgh

ONE PERSON EXHIBITION
1987 Eden Court Theatre, Inverness

GROUP EXHIBITION
1989 *Scatter*, New Scottish Art, Third Eye Centre, Glasgow*

GARY HUME 66

Born 1962, Kent

1985-86 Liverpool Polytechnic
1986-88 Goldsmiths' School of Art, London

Lives in London

Karsten Schubert Ltd, London

ONE PERSON EXHIBITION
1989 Karsten Schubert Ltd, London

GROUP EXHIBITIONS
1988 *Freeze* (Part II), London Docklands
Ian Davenport, Gary Hume, Michael Landy, Karsten Schubert Ld, London
1989 Painting Show. Lorence Monk Gallery, New York.
Angela Bulloch, Gary Hume, Michael Landy, Esther Schipper, Cologne
1990 *A Painting Show: Michael Craig-Martin, Gary Hume, Christopher Wool*, Karsten Schubert Ltd, London

KABIR HUSSAIN 68

Born 1960, Nara, Pakistan

1979-80 Jacob Kramer College, Leeds
1980-83 South Glamorgan Institute of Higher Education, Cardiff
1983-84 Chelsea School of Art, London

Lives in Cardiff

AWARDS
1984 Henry Moore Foundation Prize
1985 Setting-up Grant, Welsh Arts Council
1988 Travel grant, Welsh Arts Council

ONE PERSON EXHIBITIONS
1988 National Eisteddfod, Newport
Landscape, Llanover Hall, Cardiff
1989 Installation, Bute Park, Cardiff

SELECTED GROUP EXHIBITIONS
1984 *Christie's Inaugural*, London
London Group '84
1985 *Ex-Jacob Kramer Students 1979-1980/1980-81*, Leeds*
1987 Lower Machen Festival*
One Journey, Two Expressions, Cardiff*
Chapter Artists, Pontypridd Cultural Centre

BETHAN HUWS 70

Born 1961, Bangor, Wales

1981-85 Middlesex Polytechnic, London
1986-88 Royal College of Art, London

Lives in London

Anthony Reynolds Gallery, London

ONE PERSON EXHIBITIONS
1987   Institut Sainte-Marie, Brussels*
1988   Rivington Street, London
            Anthony Reynolds Gallery, London
1989   Riverside Studios, London
            FRAC des Pays de la Loire, Garenne Lemot,
            Clisson*

CALLUM INNES 72

Born 1962, Edinburgh

1980-84   Gray's School of Art, Aberdeen
1984-85   Edinburgh College of Art

Lives in Edinburgh

AWARDS
1983   Shell Expo Premier Prize, Aberdeen Artists
1984   Hospital Field Summer Scholarship
            Hector Memorial Travelling Scholarship
1987-88   Scottish Arts Council, Amsterdam Residency

ONE PERSON EXHIBITIONS
1986   Artspace Gallery, Aberdeen
1988   369 Gallery, Edinburgh

SELECTED GROUP EXHIBITIONS
1983-87   Aberdeen Artists
1984   Transmission Gallery, Glasgow
1984-85   Scottish Young Contemporaries Travelling
            Exhibition
1985   Artspace Galleries
            Smith Biennial, Stirling
1985-87   Paisley Drawing Biennial
1986   Selection from Smith at Third Eye Centre,
            Glasgow
            Selection at Warwick Arts Trust, London*
            Group Show Collective, Edinburgh
            Greenock Biennial
1988   369 Gallery, Edinburgh
1989   369 Gallery, Edinburgh
            Scatter, Third Eye Centre, Glasgow*
            Smith Biennial, Stirling*

BRIAN W. JENKINS 74

Born 1964, Falkirk

1982-84   Falkirk College of Technology
1984-88   Glasgow School of Art

Lives in Falkirk

AWARDS
1984-88   BP Education Trust, Scholarship Awards

SELECTED GROUP EXHIBITIONS
1987-88   Student Exhibitions, Newbery Gallery, Glasgow
            School of Art
1987   Third Eye Centre, Glasgow
            Joint Artist Book Exhibition, Royal Scottish
            Academy, Edinburgh
1988   Family, My History, Myself, United Gallery,
            Sheffield, Plymouth Arts Centre and Ffotogallery,
            Cardiff, Stills Gallery, Edinburgh
            Performance/Instatllation, The National Review of
            Live Art, Glasgow*
1988   Joint Artist Book Exhibition, Graeme Murray
            Gallery, Edinburgh*
            Open Land, Portfolio Gallery, Edinburgh*
            The Square Gallery, London
            Contemporary '88, The Dick Institute, Kilmarnock
1989   Through Photography, Third Eye Centre,
            Glasgow*

PATRICK KEILLER 76

Born 1950, Blackpool, Lancs

1967-79   Studied and practised architecture
1979-81   Royal College of Art London, Department of
            Environmental Media

FILMS
1981   Stonebridge Park, 16mm bw 21 mins
1981-84   Norwood, 16mm bw 26 mins, made with Arts
            Council support
1983-86   The End, 16mm bw 18 mins, made with Arts
            Council support, then to Channel Four's The
            Eleventh Hour.
1987   Valtos, 16mm bw 11 mins, for Channel Four's
            Ghosts in the Machine
1988-89   The Clouds, 16mm bw 20 mins, for the British Film
            Institute and Channel Four Television

SELECTED GROUP EXHIBITIONS AND SCREENINGS
1982   Drawings, Sound and Tape-Slide, Tate Gallery,
            London*
1984   Surrealist Film Season, London Film-makers'
            Co-op*
            Cross-Currents, Ten Years of Mixed Media, Royal
            College of Art London Film Festival*
1985   The New Pluralism, Tate Gallery, London*
1986   London Film Festival*
            Edinburgh International Film Festival*
1986-87   Charting Time: Drawings for Film and Video,
            Serpentine Gallery, London and Hatton Gallery,
            Newcastle-upon-Tyne*
            Heroic Times, Tour of 1920s Soviet and French
            with recent British Experimental film*
1987   Recent Experimental Film in Britain, Budapest
            The Elusive Sign, British Avant-garde Film and
            Video, 1977-87, British Council International
            Tour*
1988   National Film Theatre, London*
            UKLA, Los Angeles

The Watershed, Bristol
Complete Works, ICA Cinematheque, London
Melbourne Film Festival, Certificate of Merit*
Ösnabruck Film Festival
1989   Krakow Film Festival
Metro Cinema, London*
Edinburgh International Film Festival
Tyneside Film Festival
Birmingham Film Festival
Leeds Film Festival
Turin Film Festival

JOANNA KIRK   78

Born 1963, Cheshire

1981-84   Goldsmiths' College of Art, London

Lives in London

Nicola Jacobs Gallery, London

Awards
1987   Joint First Prize, 1987 Artist Award, Whitechapel
Art Gallery, London

ONE PERSON EXHIBITIONS
1987   Third Eye Centre, Glasgow
Nicola Jacobs Gallery, London
1988   New Gallery, Whitechapel Art Gallery, London*
1989   Carine Campo Gallery, Antwerp
Nicola Jacobs Gallery, London

SELECTED GROUP EXHIBITIONS
1984   Christie's Inaugural Exhibition, London
Riverside Studios, London
1986   Love: Sacred and Profane, Plymouth Arts Centre
Interference, Riverside Studios, London*
1987   Group Show, Richard Pomeroy Gallery, London
1988   Vanitas, Norwich School of Art Gallery,
Norwich*
1989   Selections from the Collections of M. Anwar
Kamal Twentieth-Century Drawing and Sculpture,
Cummer Gallery of Art, Jacksonville, Florida
Subject: Object, Nicola Jacobs Gallery, London

ELIZABETH MAGILL   80

Born 1959, Ontario, Canada

1979-82   Belfast College of Art, Northern Ireland
1982-84   Slade School of Art, London

Lives in London

RESIDENCIES AND AWARDS
1982   Arts Council of Northern Ireland Bursary Award
1983   Guinness Peat Aviation Award
Alice Berger Hammerschlag Travel Award
1984   Boise Travel Scholarship
GP Robinson Award

1985   The Jacob Mendleson Trust Grant
Artist in Residence, Portsmouth College of Art
1986   Arts Council of Northern Ireland Bursary Award
1989   Arts Council of Northern Ireland Bursary Award

ONE PERSON EXHIBITIONS
1987   Kerlin Gallery, Belfast
1989   Kerlin Gallery, Dublin*
Anolfini Gallery, Bristol*

SELECTED GROUP EXHIBITIONS
1983   Stowells Trophy Exhibition, Royal Academy,
London
Guiness Peat Aviation Awards for Emerging
Artists, Douglas Hyde Gallery, Dublin
1984   Christie's Inaugural, London
Royal College of Art, London
David Hendricks Gallery, Dublin
1985   Riverside Open, Riverside Studios, London
David Hendricks Gallery, Dublin
1988   Ulster Artists in the '80s, R.H.A. Gallery, Dublin
Kerlin Gallery, Dublin
5 London Artists, Nancy Hoffmann Gallery, New
York
1989   Kerlin Gallery, Dublin

LISA MILROY   82

Born 1959, Vancouver, Canada

1976   Banff School of Fine Art, Alberta, Canada
1977-78 L'Universite de la Sorbonne, Paris
1978-79 St Martin's School of Art, London
1979-82 Goldsmiths' College of Art, London

Lives in London

Nicola Jacobs Gallery, London

AWARDS
1989   First Prize, John Moores Liverpool Exhibition 16,
Walker Art Gallery, Liverpool

ONE PERSON EXHIBITIONS
1984   Nicola Jacobs Gallery, London
Cartier Art Foundation, Paris*
1986   Nicola Jacobs Gallery, London
Khiva Gallery, San Francisco
1988   Nicola Jacobs Gallery, London
1989   John Burggruen Gallery, San Francisco
Third Eye Centre, Glasgow, Southampton City Art
Gallery, Plymouth Art Gallery*
Mary Boone Gallery, New York

SELECTED GROUP SHOWS
1983   Charterhouse Gallery, London
Young Blood, Riverside Studios, London
1984   Problems of Picturing, Serpentine Gallery, London
1985   John Moores Liverpool Exhibition 14, Walker Art
Gallery, Liverpool
1986   Sixth Sydney Biennale

Aperto, Venice Biennale
Japonisme, Northern Centre for Contemporary
Art, Sunderland
Au Coeur du Maelstrom, Palais des Beaux Arts,
Brussels
Objects as Art, Plymouth Arts Centre
No Place Like Home, Cornerhouse, Manchester
1987   *Winter '87*, Nicola Jacobs Gallery, London
John Moores Liverpool Exhibition 15. Walker Art
Gallery, Liverpool
Current Affairs: British Painting and Sculpture in
the 1980s, (touring Eastern Europe), Museum of
Modern Art, Oxford
British Art of the 1980s: 1987, Sweden and
Finland, British Council tour
Cries and Whispers: Paintings of the 1980s from
the British Council Collection, touring Australia
and New Zealand
1987-88 *Three Artists from Britain*, Jack Shainman Gallery,
Washington DC and New York
1988   *Winter '88*, Nicola Jacobs Gallery, London
New British Painting, Contemporary Art Centre,
Cincinatti and USA tour
1989   Art of the '80s, from the Collection of Chemical
Bank, the Montclair Art Museum, Montclair, New
Jersey
Lisa Milroy, Tony Cragg, John Murphy, Pierides
Museum of Contemporary Art, Athens
Subject: Object, Nicola Jacobs Gallery, London
John Moores Liverpool Exhibition 16, Walker Art
Gallery, Liverpool

JOHN MITCHELL 84

Born 1953, Glasgow

Lives in London

1974-78 Edinburgh College of Art
1977   Summer School, Yale University, USA
1979-80 Goldsmiths' College, London
1984-85 Art Teachers' Certificate Course, Goldsmiths'
College
1989   Institute of Education, London

ONE PERSON EXHIBITIONS
1986   *Wounded and Torn*, Interim Art, London Foyer,
Riverside Studios, London
1987   HANDLE WITH CARE/DO NOT CRUSH, Unit 7
Gallery, London Occurrences, Seagate Gallery,
Dundee

TWO PERSON EXHIBITIONS
1981   Mercer Union Gallery, Toronto, Canada
1986   A John Hansard Gallery Touring Exhibition, The
Gantry, Southampton.

GROUP EXHIBITIONS
1977   Printmakers' Workshop, Edinburgh, Scotland
Yale University Art Gallery, Norfolk, Connecticut,
UWA

1980   New Contemporaries, ICA, London
Nine Scottish Artists, The Hatton Gallery,
University of Newcastle-upon-Tyne
1985   Richard Demarco Gallery, 2nd International
Contemporary Art Flair, Olympia, London
Brixton Art Gallery, London
Richard Demarco Gallery, Bath Contemporary Art
Fair
New Moon Studios, Ladywell Baths, Lewisham,
London
1986   Open Studios, New Moon Studios, Catford,
London
Out of Dereliction, Woodlands Art Gallery,
London
Gold, Frankincense and Myrrh, Adam Gallery,
London
1987   21st Anniversary Exhibition, Richard Demarco
Gallery, Smith's Galleries, London
New Moon Artists, New Moon Studios, Catford,
London
New Moon Studios, Woodlands Art Gallery,
London
New Moon Studios, Open Studio Weekend,
Catford, London
Grey Matter New Sculpture 88, Ikon Gallery,
Birmingham
1988   The Dynamo, Unit 7 Gallery, London

LOCKY MORRIS 56

Locky Morris was born in Derry in 1960 where he continues to
live and work. He doesn't work as an isolated individual but in
collaboration with the collective experience and history of his
community. His sculptures represent the experience and hopes
of Derry people living in the most militarized zone in Western
Europe.

Locky Morris, November 1989

JULIAN OPIE 86

Born 1958, London

1979-82 Goldsmiths' School of Art, London

Lives in London

Lisson Gallery, London

ONE PERSON EXHIBITIONS
1983   Lisson Gallery, London
1984   "Perspective '84", Internationale Kunstmesse, Basel
Kolnischer Kunstmesse, Basel Kolnischer
Kunstverein, Cologne*
1985   Groninger Museum, Groningen
Lisson Gallery, London*
1986   Drawings 1982 to 1985, ICA, Camden
Franco Toselli Gallery, Milan
Lisson Gallery, London
1988   Lisson Gallery, London*

Galeria Montenegro, Madrid
Gallery Paul Maenz, Cologne

SELECTED GROUP EXHIBITIONS

1982   Lisson Gallery, London
Sculpture for a Garden, (Hounslow Sculpture II),
Gunnersbury Park, London

1983   Charterhouse Square, London
Young Blood, Riverside Studios, London
Beelden '83, Rotterdam Arts Council, Rotterdam*
The Sculpture Show, Hayward Gallery/
Serpentine Gallery, London*
8 Sculptor's Drawings, Air Gallery, London
Tate Gallery Making Sculpture, Making Sculpture,
Tate Gallery, London

1984   *Underwater*, Plymouth Arts Centre
Sculpture Symposeum 1984, St Jean-Port, Quebec
Metaphor and/or Symbol, The National Museum
of Modern Art, Tokyo & The National Museum of
Art, Osaka*
William Morris Today, ICA, London

1985   *The British Show*, Art Gallery of Western
Australia, Perth and Australia/New Zealand tour*
Still Life: A New Life, Harris Museum and Art
Gallery, Preston, and tour
Anniottanta, Assessorato alla Cultura del
Commune di Ravenna, Italy*
Three British Sculptors, The Israel Museum,
Jerusalem*
Place Saint Lambert Investigations, Espace Nord,
Liege*
Figure 1, Aberystwyth Arts Centre, Wales
The Irresistible Object — Still Life 1600-1985,
Leeds City Art Galleries
Sculpture In a Garden, Bluecoat Gallery,
Liverpool

1986   *Forty years of Modern Art 1945-1985*, Tate
gallery, London*
Sculpture — 9 Artists from Britain, Louisiana
Museum, Humlebaek, Denmark*
XVII Triennale de Milano, Italy and Grand Palais,
Paris*
Englische Bildhauer, Galerie Harald Behm,
Hamburg
Prospect '86, Frankfurt*
Correspondence Europe, Stedelijk Museum,
Amsterdam*

1986-90 *Focus on the Image: Selection from the Rivendell
Collection*, circulated by the Art Museum
Association of America

1987   *British Art of the 1980s: 1987*, Liljevalchs
Konsthall, Stockholm, & Sara Hilden Museum,
Tampere, Finland, British Council tour
Casting an Eye, Cornerhouse, Manchester
Fuller Goldeen Gallery, San Francisco

1988   *Europa Oggi*, Inaugural Exhibition, Museo d'Arte
Contemporanea, Prato, Italy*
Les Années 80: A la surface de la Peinture, Centre
d'Art Contemporain, Abbaye Saint-Andre,
Maymac
Wolff Gallery, New York

1988-89 *Britannica: Trente Ans de Sculpture*, Musee des
Beaux Arts Andre Malraux, Le Havre and tour*
British Sculpture 1960-1988, Museum van
Hedendaugse Kunst, Antwerp*

1989   Lia Rumma Gallery, Naples
Mediated Knot, Robin Lockett Gallery, Chicago*
Object/Objectif, Galerie Daniel Templon, Paris*
Skulptur Teil 11, Galerie Six Friedrich, Munich
D. &S. Hamburg Kunstverein, Hamburg*

1990   *Objectives: The New Sculpture*, Newport Harbor
Art Museum, California*

CORNELIA PARKER   88

Born 1956, Cheshire

1974-75   Gloucestershire College of Art and Design
1975-78   Wolverhampton Polytechnic
1980-82   Reading University

Lives in London

AWARDS, COMMISSIONS AND RESIDENCIES

1978   Wolverhampton Polytechnic Travel Scholarship
1979-80 Artist in Residence, Crewe and Alsager College
1983   Southern Arts Award
1985   Greater London Arts Award
1986   National Garden Festival, Stoke-on-Trent,
Sculpture Commission
Siteworks Commission Installation around Borough
Market
1988   Sculpture Residency and Commission, Forest of
Dean,
Thirty Pieces of Silver, Ikon Gallery commissionm,
Birmingham
1989   *Left Luggage*, Edge '90 commission, St. Pancras
station

ONE PERSON EXHIBITIONS

1980   Alsager Arts Centre Gallery
1981   Stoke City Art Gallery & Museum
1983   Hexagon, Reading
1987   Actualites, London*
1988-89 *Thirty Pieces of Silver*, Ikon Gallery, Birmingham
and Aspex Gallery, Portsmouth*
1989   *Matter and What It Means*, Cornerhouse,
Manchester*

SELECTED GROUP EXHIBITIONS

1979   *Four Polytechnics*, Chester Arts Centre
1980   *Midland View*, Stoke City Art Gallery and touring
1983   Reading/Dusseldorf Studio Exchange Show
Sculpture by Women, Ikon Gallery, Birmingham
Ikon Touring Drawing Exhibition
1985   *Whitechapel Open*, London
1986   *Surveying the Scene*, South Hill Park, Bracknell
and Aspex Gallery, Portsmouth*
New British Sculpture, Air Gallery, London*
No Place Like Home, Cornerhouse, Manchester*
1987   *Work for Shelves — A System of Support*, Kettle's
Yard, Cambridge

VONGPHRACHANH PHAOPHANIT   90

Born 1961, Savannahket, Laos

1980-82   Ecole des Beaux Arts, Aix en Provence, France
1982-85   Aix en Provence, BA Fine Art

Lives in Bristol

ONE PERSON EXHIBITIONS
1986   *On All Fours*, Bennets Shop, Brighton Festival
       Aqua Pittura, Espace Sextius, Aix en Provence, France*
       One Coat Amongst Others, Red Herring Gallery, Brighton
1987   *Fleeting Monuments*, Brighton Festival*
       Just a Moment, Spacex Gallery, Exeter
1988   *Just a Moment*, Chapter Art Centre, Cardiff

SELECTED GROUP EXHIBITIONS
1987   *Tea Ceremony*, with Situation Cinema, Cardiff Art College
       If Looks Could Kill, Red Herring Gallery, Brighton
1988   *Patron,-onne*, with Situation Cinema, Red Herring Gallery
       Leonardo Seduce Me, with Situation Cinema, Brighton Festival
       One Coat Amongst Others, Red Herring Gallery, Brighton
       Traffic, with Time Lapse, Garage Site, Bristol
1989   Group Show, with Time Lapse, Third Eye Centre, Glasgow.
       Mixed media installation with Ouverture, Amsterdam, Holland*
       The Artist Abroad, Usher Gallery, Lincoln

Work in the exhibition realised with the help of Xpelair

FIONA RAE   92

Born 1963, Hong Kong

1983-4   Foundation Course, Croydon College
1984-7   BA Honours Fine Art, Goldsmiths' College, London

Lives in London

SELECTED GROUP EXHIBITIONS
1988   Freeze, London Docklands*
1989   Anderson O'Day Gallery, London
       Promises Promises, Serpentine Gallery, London, Ecole de Nimes, France*

DAVID ROBILLIARD   94

Born 1952, died 1988

Friedman-Guinness Gallery, Frankfurt

EXHIBITIONS AND PUBLICATIONS
1984   Stephen Bartley Ltd., London
       Inevitable, book of poems published by Gilbert & George, London
1985   James Birch Fine Art, London
1986   Art & Project, Amsterdam, Holland
       Bulletin of poems, sent out by direct mail, published by Art & Project, Amsterdam (repeated 1988)
1987   Van Abbe Museum, Eindhoven, Holland
       Swallowing Helmets, book of poems published by Van Abbe Museum, Eindhoven
       Mailing of monthly poetry cards, published by Birch & Conran (continued 1988)
       Galerie Hufkens-Noirhomme, Brussels, Belgium
       Birch & Conran Fine Art, London
       Friedman-Guinness Gallery, Heidelberg
1988   Artist of the Day, Angela Flowers Gallery, London
1989   Friedman-Guinness Gallery, Frankfurt
1990   Tom Cugliani Gallery, New York
       Baby Lies Truthfully, book of poems published by Inanout Press, New York/ Rome
       Life Isn't Good — It's Excellent, book of poems published by Gilbert & George, London

CAROLINE RUSSELL   96

Born 1962, Aldershot

1980-83   Ruskin School of Art, Oxford University
1986-88   Goldsmiths' School of Art, London
1989-90   Fellowship, Goldsmiths' MA Site Tutor

Lives in London

ONE PERSON EXHIBITIONS
1988   Anthony Reynolds Gallery, London
1989   *Display 21*, Chisenhale Gallery, London

SELECTED GROUP EXHIBITIONS
1984   *New Sculpture in Oxford*, St Paul's Art Centre, Oxford
       City Sculpture, Ikon Gallery Workspace, Birmingham
1985   *Women and Towers*, Partridge Works, Birmingham
1986   Group Show, Chisenhale Gallery, London
1988   *19&&*, Magasin, Centre National D'Art Contemporain, Grenoble, France*
       Grey Matter, Ikon Gallery*
       Whitechapel Open, London
       Show & Tell, Riverside Studios, London*
1989   *Concept 88 Reality 89*, Essex University*
       Europa 92: Fields of Vision, Zenit Deposito d'Arte, Turin, Italy*

Work in the exhibition realised with the help of Stephenson Evitt Systems Ltd and Europack Engineering Company, manufacturers of Ridat Machines

VERONICA RYAN   98

Born 1956, Plymouth, Montserrat,

1974-75   St. Albans College of Art and Design
1975-78   Bath Academy of Art
1978-80   The Slade School of Art, University College,
          London
1981-83   The School of Oriental and African Studies

Lives in London

AWARDS
1980   Boise Travelling Scholarship
1983   GLA Awards Second Prize Winner, Cleveland
          (UK) International Drawing Biennale
1985   GLA Award
1987   Henry Moore Foundation Award

ONE PERSON EXHIBITIONS
1984   *Drawings and Sculpture*, the Tom Allen Centre,
          London
          Drawings, South of the Border Restaurant, London
1987   Arnolfini Gallery, Bristol and touring to
          Wolverhampton City Art Gallery and Third Eye
          centre, Glasgow*
1988   Kettle's Yard, Cambridge and Riverside Studios,
          London*

SELECTED GROUP EXHIBITIONS
1981   *Third World Show*, London School of Economics
1982   *Fine Art Staff Show*, Aspex Gallery, Portsmouth
1983   The Showroom, London
          Black Women Time Now, Battersea Arts Centre,
          London
          Five Black Women Artists, The Africa Centre,
          London
          Creation for Liberation, Brixton, Sixth Cleveland
          International Drawing Biennale, and touring
          The Gallery, Acre Lane, Brixton
1984   *Sculptors and Modellers*, Tate Gallery, London*
          The Mappin Art Gallery, Sheffield
          The Elizabeth Gallery, London
1985   *The Thin Black Line*, ICA, London*
          Manna in the Wilderness, Angela Flowers
          Gallery, London
          William Morris Museum, Walthamstow, London*
          The Whitechapel Open, Whitechapel Art Gallery,
          London
          New Horizons, Royal Festival Hall, London
1986   *From Two Worlds*, Whitechapel Art Gallery,
          London*
          Interim Art, London
          The Minories, Colchester
          Caribbean Expressions in Britain, Leicester
          Museums and Art Gallery
          Four London Artists, Oriel Theatre, Clwyd, North
          Wales
          Whitechapel Open, Whitechapel Art Gallery,
          London
          Stoke City Garden Festival, Stoke on Trent
          Coloured Sculpture, Stoke on Trent Museum and
          Art Gallery;
          Blond Fine Art, London
1987   *Vessels*, Serpentine Art Gallery, London
          Works for Shelves: A System of Support, Kettle's
          Yard, Cambridge
          Dislocations, Kettle's Yard, Cambridge*
1988   *Inside Out*, Nottingham Castle Museum
          In the Close, Jesus College, Cambridge
1989   *Sculpture in a Rose Garden*. St Albans, Chiswell
          Green, Herts. *

LESLEY SANDERSON   100

Born 1962

1980-81   West Surrey College of Art & Design
1981-84   Sheffield City Polytechnic

Lives in Sheffield

SELECTED GROUP EXHIBITIONS
1984-5   *Sheffield Open*, Mappin Gallery
1985   *South Yorkshire Open*, Barnsley Art Gallery
1986   *New Contemporaries*, ICA London & Bluecoat
          Liverpool*
          City Life, Political Life, Private Life, Public Life,
          The Cornerhouse, Manchester*
1987   New Art in Yorkshire, Leeds
          Witness, New Art in Sheffield
1988   *Current Work; A Reputation Amongst Artists*,
          Graves Art Gallery, Sheffield*
          Separate Perceptions, St. Paul's gallery, Leeds
          Intercity '88, Birmingham & Sheffield
1988-89   *Black Art — Plotting the Course*, Oldham Gallery
          & tour*
          Along the Lines of Resistance, Cooper Gallery,
          Barnsley & Rochdale Art Gallery*
1989   *North by Northwest*, the B.B.K Cologne,
          Germany*
1990   *Let the Canvas Come to Life with Dark Faces*,
          Contemporary Non-European Self-Portrait,
          Herbert Art Gallery, Coventry*

LOUISE SCULLION   102

Born 1966, Helensburgh

1984-88   Glasgow School of Art
1988   Cargill Travelling Scholarship

Lives in Helensburgh

RESIDENCIES
1989   Artist in Residence, Smith Art Gallery & Museum

ONE PERSON EXHIBITIONS
1988   *Just Another Outdoor Game*, Third Eye Centre,
          Glasgow
1990   Compass Gallery, Glasgow*

1988   *Exhibition of Women Artists*, Strathclyde
University; Glasgow Garden Festival;
Group Exhibition, Crawford Centre for the Arts

1989   *The Soft Machine*, Printmakers' Gallery, Glasgow
Scatter, Third Eye Centre, Glasgow*

YOLANDE SNAITH   104

Born 1960, Sutton, Surrey

1977-79   Wimbledon School of Art
Central School of Art
1979-83   Dartington College of Arts

Lives in London

AWARDS
1988   Digital Dance Award
GLA Dance Award
1989   Digital Dance Award
London 'Time Out and Dance Umbrella' Dance
and Performance Award

PERFORMANCE AND CHOREOGRAPHY
1984   *Domestic Demonstrations, for You I Would Do
Anything, Mover*, performed at Dance Umbrella,
Chisenhale Dance Space, Rotherhithe Theatre
Workshop, Zap Club, Brighton
1985   *Thou Shalt Not*, Riverside Studios, London and
Dartington Dance Festival
Blue-Whiteness Rhapsody, Crouch End Festival,
Laban Centre, London & Dance Umbrella
Out of the Action, Chisenhale Dance Space &
Dance Umbrella Space
As Thing As Things, performance with Ken Turner,
Midland Group, Nottingham & Zap Club,
Brighton
1986   Dance/Film collaboration, *Soh-Fa*, with Simon
Casel, October Gallery, London, Old Bull Arts
Centre, London, Dartington Dance Festival & The
Premises, Norwich
The Bitch and the Wardrobe, with Michelle
Richcoeur, The Place Theatre, London
Dancer with Extemporary Dance Theatre
Scared Shirtless & fresco Fresco, ICA, London,
British and foreign tour
1987   *Conceptual Clothing*, Ikon Gallery and British tour
Extract from *Scared Shirtless* filmed for Omnibus,
BBC Television; Step In Time Girls, film
collaboration with Terry Braun, for Channel Four
Television
1988   *Can Baby Jane Can Can*, premiered at the Place
Theatre and Waterman's Arts Centre, London,
British and foreign tour
Excerpts featured on 01 for London
1989   *The Hunt*, Collaboration with students at Leicester
Polytechnic, Leicester International Dance Festival
Lessons in Social Skills, Lancaster Nuffield Theatre
& The Place Theatre, London. Later extended to
become:

Germs: Advanced Lessons in Social Skills, together
with film with Peter Carlton — British and foreign
tour

GARY STEVENS   106

Born 1953, London

1971-73   East Ham College of Technology
1973-76   Goldsmiths' School of Art
1981-83   Slade School of Fine Art

Lives in London

ONE PERSON PERFORMANCE
1984   *Imagining Applying Pressure to the Flaw*,
Southampton Art Gallery
1985-86   *Invisible Work*,
Acme Studios, London
Goldsmiths' School of Art
Museum of Modern Art, Oxford
Midland Group, Nottingham
Assembly Rooms, Edinburgh
Laing Art Gallery, Newcastle
ICA Theatre, London
Ikon Gallery, Birmingham
1986-87   *If The Cap Fits*,
Acme Studios
Faculty of Art & Design, Cardiff
Goldsmiths' School of Art
Southampton Art Gallery
ICA Theatre
Trent Polytechnic, Nottingham
Medway College of Design, Rochester
St. Botolph's Church, London
Chapter, Cardiff
Kettle's Yard, Cambridge
St. Martin's School of Art, London
Whitechapel Art Gallery, London
Castle Museum, Nottingham
Assembly Rooms, Edinburgh
Third Eye Centre, Glasgow
The Leadmill, Sheffield
Arnolfini, Bristol
St. Donat's Arts Centre, South Wales
Town Hall Studio, Swindon
Prema, Gloucestershire
1987-88   Sydney Biennale
Different Ghosts, ICA Theatre
Traverse Theatre, Edinburgh
ICA Theatre
Trent Polytechnic
Chapter Arts Centre
South Hill Park Arts Centre
Pegasus, Oxford
Green Rooms, Manchester
Brewery Arts Centre, Kendal

PERFORMANCE WITH STATION HOUSE OPERA
1983-84   ICA Theatre

Midland Group, Nottingham
Brighton Festival
International Festival of Performance, South Hill
Park Arts Centre, Bracknell
Centre, Bracknell
GLC Festival, London
The British Art Show, Birmingham, Edinburgh,
Southampton, Sheffield*
Bloomsbury Theatre, London

LINDA TAYLOR   108

Born 1959, Scotland

1976-80   Edinburgh College of Art

Lives in Glasgow

ONE PERSON EXHIBITIONS
1985   Collective Gallery, Edinburgh
1987   Graeme Murray Gallery, Edinburgh

SELECTED GROUP EXHIBITIONS
1981   *Contemporary Abstraction*, Fruitmarket Gallery,
        Edinburgh*
1983   *Women Live in Scotland*, Belford Church,
        Edinburgh*
        Graeme Murray Gallery, Edinburgh
1984   *Four Artists*, Transmission Gallery, Glasgow
        Wasps Gallery, Edinburgh
1985   *Peace Festival*, Kelvinhall, Glasgow
1986   *The Eye of the Storm*, Stirling Smith Gallery
        Touring Exhibition*
1987   *The Unpainted Landscape*, Scottish Arts Council
        Touring Exhibition*
        The State of the Nation, Herbert Art Gallery,
        Coventry*
        Trigon Biennale, The Neue Gallery, Graz,
        Austria*
1988   Glasgow Garden Festival*
        St. Peter's Church Yard, Kettle's Yard,
        Cambridge*
        Diane Brown Gallery, New York
        Graeme Murray Gallery
1989   Graeme Murray Gallery
        Scottish Art Since 1900, Scottish National Gallery
        of Modern Art, Edinburgh*
        Scatter, Third Eye Centre, Glasgow*

PETER TURLEY   110

Born 1955, London

1972-73   Goldsmiths' College, London
1974-77   Chelsea School of Art, London

Lives in Suffolk

SELECTED GROUP EXHIBITIONS
1988   *Land*, Riverside Studios, London*

SHAFIQUE UDDIN   112

Born 1962, Bangladesh

Lives in London

ONE PERSON EXHIBITIONS
1979   Whitechapel Art Gallery, London
1983   Tower Hamlets Exhibition Circuit
1985   Tower Hamlets Exhibition Circuit
1986   Salvatore Ala Gallery, New York
        Montefiore Centre, London
1988   Horizon Gallery, London

SELECTED GROUP EXHIBITIONS
1982-88   Whitechapel Open
1987-88   *In Another World*, South Bank Centre Touring
           Exhibition
1987   *Outsiders*, Prema Project, Gloucestershire
1988   *Celebration of Outsider Art*, Giray & Monolith,
           London

RACHEL WHITEREAD   114

Born 1963, London

1982-85   Brighton Polytechnic
1985-87   Slade School of Art

Lives in London

AWARDS
1989   The Elephant Trust

ONE PERSON EXHIBITIONS
1988   Carlile Gallery, London
1990   Chisenhale Gallery, London

SELECTED GROUP EXHIBITIONS
1987   *Whitworth Young Contemporaries*, Manchester
1988   *Riverside Open*, London
        Slaughterhouse Gallery, London
1989   *Concept 88 Reality 89*, University of Essex
        Gallery*
        Whitechapel Open, London
        Einleuchten: Will, Vorstel und Simul in HH,
        Hamburg*

CAROLINE WILKINSON   116

Born 1951, Edinburgh

1970-75   Edinburgh University and College of Art

Lives in London

AWARDS AND RESIDENCIES
1975   Andrew Grant Travelling Scholarship
1985   Artist in Residence, Grenfell School, London
        Arts Council Grant, GLA Award

SELECTED EXHIBITIONS, SCREENINGS AND
PERFORMANCES

1976	Edinburgh College of Art
	Two Journeys/Height Slides, Theatre of Mistakes, Slade School of Fine Art, London*
	The Art Room, London
1977	The London Group, Camden Arts Centre
	The Polytechnic of North London
	The Waterfall, Theatre of Mistakes,
	Hayward Annual, Hayward Gallery, London*
1981	Brunnings, Whitechapel
1981-82	Cleveland International Drawing Biennale*
1982	London Film-Makers' Co-op
1983	ICA Cinematheque, London
	Air Gallery, London
1984	*Whitechapel Open*, London
	Downstairs, Upstairs, Camerawork, London
	The 100 Artists Show, the Showroom, London
	Six Artists, St Botolphs, Aldgate, London
1985	Whitechapel Open, London
	Interiors, Spitalfields Health Centre, London
	Leisure: Out of Work: Home Entertainment, Installation, Camerawork, London*
1986	*Whitechapel Open*, London
	The Drawing Room, London (Book 1988)*
	Consequences, tape-slide commission for Tower Hamlets
	Womens' Arts Festival, Whitechapel Art Gallery, London
	Prudence, the Daylight Club, Diorama, London*
1987	*Another Monday and School Days*, tape-slide, Whitechapel Art Gallery, London*
	School Days, Animal Vegetable Mineral and Prudence, Whitechapel Art Gallery, London
1988	Art Gallery of Western Australia, Perth
	Whitechapel Open, London
	Sound Moves, sound commission, Projects UK, Newcastle Four Minute Piece, Unit 7 Gallery, London
1985-89	Performed with Gary Stevens, *If The Cap Fits* tour*
1989	*Twilight*, installation, Unit 7 Gallery, London*

The following magazines give full and regular coverage to contemporary British art:

ART LINE
ART MONTHLY
ARTSCRIBE
ARTS REVIEW
THE BURLINGTON MAGAZINE
MODERN PAINTERS

The following magazines offer in-depth coverage of important aspects of contemporary British art:

ALBA
AND JOURNAL OF ART AND ART EDUCATION
ART AND DESIGN
ARTISTS' NEWSLETTER
CRAFTS MAGAZINE
CIRCA
ARTRAGE
CREATIVE CAMERA
BLOCK
FEMINIST ART NEWS
PERFORMANCE
PORTFOLIO
TEN 8
THIRD TEXT

These magazines, published abroad, regularly cover British art in an international context:

ARTEFACTUM (Belgium)
ARTFORUM (USA)
ART IN AMERICA (USA)
CONTEMPORANEA (Italy)
ARENA (Spain)
ART NEWS (USA)
FLASH ART (Italy)
KUNSTFORUM (Germany)
NEW ART EXAMINER (USA)
PARACHUTE (Canada)
PARKETT (Switzerland)
ART & TEXT (USA/Australia)

Selectors' Acknowledgements

We are grateful to the staff in a number of departments at the South Bank Centre, especially Wendy Hepper, who made the transcripts of long conversations with artists and, above all, Lesley McRae who has held the whole process together from the start with a combination of good humour and charm which almost belies her efficiency and hard work. We would like to thank the artists and all those people who gave us advice, help and hospitality during the selection process including, Hugh Adams, Judy Adam, Emma Anderson, Marjorie Allthorpe-Guyton, Tony Arefin, Barry Barker, John Bewley, Brian Biggs, Fionna Blackburn, Mr and Mrs Paul Bradley, Clare Brett, Les Buckingham, Stuart Cameron, Eddie Chambers, Caethe Chernay, Mike Collier, Lynne Cooke, Michael Craig-Martin, Celia Cross, David Curtis, Peter Davies, Richard Deacon, Yvonne Deane, Gerald Deslandes, Micky Donnelly, Terry Duffy, Katherine Eustace, Lindsay Gordon, Esther Friedman, Linda Graham, Linda Galbraith, John Gillett, Rosy Greenleas, Hilary Gresty, Anna Harding, Jane Heath, Simon Herbert, Susanna Heron, Tom Heslop, Damien Hirst, Isabel Hitchman, Alan Humberstone, Chrissie Iles, Tessa Jackson, Peter Jones, Victoria Keller, Chris Kennedy, Angela Kingston, Monika Kinley, Robin Klasnik, Caroline Krzesinska, Sotiris Kyriacou, David Lawson, Catherine Lampert, Michael Langley, Jem Legh, James Lingwood, Robert Livingston, Alan Livingston, Amanda Loosemore, Euan McArthur, Elizabeth MacCrae, Martha McCullock, Bob McGilvery, Declan McGonagle, Elizabeth McGregor, Moira McIver, John MacKechnie, Ian McKeever, Tracy McKenna, Bruce Maclean, Maureen Mackin, David Manley, Caroline Martin, Nikki Milican, Wendy Millard, Val Millington, Alexander Moffat, Jill Morgan, Sandy Nairne, John O'Connor, Michael O'Donnell, Michael O'Pray, Charles Quick, Robert Palmer, Steven Partridge, James Peto, Jayne Purdy, Christine Ross, Julie Seddon-Jones, Nicholas and Angela Serota, Sarah Shalgosky, Zoe Shearman, Sarah Shott, Stephen Snoddy, Ann Stuart, Mike Stubbs, Liz Tagg, Virginia Tandy, Staff at the Third Eye Centre, Glasgow, Jon Thompson, Mike Tooby, Jenni Walwin, Nigel Walsh, Tony Warcus, Sarah Wason, Arthur Watson, Vanessa Webb, Richard Wentworth, Jez Welch, Alison Wilding, Nicola White, Margaret Woodhead, Christopher Woodward

CC
AN
DW

The Outsider Archive (of
Outsider Art) London

The Outsider Archive (of
Outsider Art) London